Three Caravans to Yuma

A Bactrian Camel Train

Discovered by Paul Ullman, this rare photograph depicting Bactrian camels provokes numerous questions, and is examined in Appendix 3, herein. This photograph reproduced with the permission of Roscoe Willson.

Three Caravans to Yuma

The Untold Story
of Bactrian Camels
in Western America

by
Harlan D. Fowler

THE ARTHUR H. CLARK COMPANY
Glendale, California 1980

To my dear wife
Dᴏʀᴏᴛʜʏ
for her encouragements

Contents

Illustrations

Foreword

The frontispiece illustration showing the long line of a Bactrian camel caravan is the only one of its kind uncovered by this search for the elusive trails by which these animals traveled in western America.

Between 1860 and 1875 camels were used in the wilderness areas of most of the West. However, few of the small western towns had the luxury of a local press which typified Victoria, British Columbia; Helena, Montana; Salt Lake City, Utah; Virginia City, Nevada; and Tucson, Arizona. These towns were 500 miles apart, in areas where the military had forts to protect emigrants and commercial enterprises. Unfortunately, most of the early newspaper editions published in these localities have long since disappeared because of fire, flood and other calamities, making research for this or any such work difficult.

In my earlier work, *Camels to California,* I briefly mentioned Otto Esche's purchase of Bactrians in Siberia. This has turned out to be a more intriguing venture than the story of Uncle Sam's employment of dromedaries, and led to the discovery of Frank Laumeister, who first used the Bactrians in the Cariboo mining districts of British Columbia, and was a worthy historical figure in his own right.

This study reveals for the first time that there were three independent camel enterprises which ended up in Arizona. Of the three owners who entered that state with their charges, two of them died in Yuma, one in 1866, the other in 1891. Between these years two caravans finally entered Mexico to work the mines in Central Chihuahua.

When the Nevada State Legislature passed a law in 1875 prohibiting camels to run at large along public highways, it spelled the end not only of Uncle Sam's dromedaries but also of Otto Esche's Bactrians, which were subsequently taken to Arizona.

This writer has spent more time writing to librarians, historical societies, museums, and individuals in search of scattered information than he did in writing this book. There appears to be an astonishing lack of interest in the camels during those years, and this certainly applies to photographic records. Dozens of historical books were reviewed, all dealing with the westward movement, and in most, nary a word or sketch appeared, except as given here. It would seem that the last word on the Bactrian experiment ends with this book.

I am especially grateful to Henry Welcome and Mary Eberle for their assistance in the final coordination and stylistic preparation of this material.

HARLAN D. FOWLER
Solvang, California

Introduction

One of the most curious tales of the Bactrian camels in the United States begins in Asia with two French priests, Regis-Evariste Huc and Joseph Gabet. Their book, *Travels in Tartary, Thibet and China, 1844-1846* gave one of the first reports of how Bactrians were used. After its publication it became a well-known book and sparked an interest in the possibility of camels working in pack trains.

The two priests undertook a trip through Asia to evangelize, and clearly in Abbe Huc's case, to write a book and lecture on his travels. Both men were Lazarist priests, Gabet the elder of the two, but it was Huc who suffered ill health after the trip and returned to France. There he resigned the congregation, remarking that "community life is incompatible with my temperament."[1] In 1850, Abbe Huc gave the literate world the story of his trip, including information about Bactrians which he had gathered.

To begin with, the camel at birth requires great care and attention. For the first week of its life it can neither stand nor suck without help because of its long neck. Unlike the colt and kid, says Huc, the camel young do not play but are from birth "grave, melancholy,

---

[1] Huc, Regis-Evariste and Joseph Gabet, *Travels in Tartary, Thibet and China, 1844-1846*, Trans. by William Hazlitt (Harper and Bros., N.Y., 1928). A copy of this booklet may be obtained on loan from the State Library in Sacramento. All succeeding quotes from Huc in the introduction are from this book.

and slow," often crying in the night like an "infant in pain." The young camel seems to feel that "joy or recreation is not within its portion; that its inevitable career is forced labour and long fastings, until death shall relieve it."

Compared to other beasts of burden, the camel is long in maturing. Until it is three, it cannot even carry a single rider, and it does not reach its peak of vigor until the age of about eight. Its first test as a burden bearer begins with small loads. If it can rise with a load, it can carry that amount on a considerable journey. Given periodic rests during the year, the Abbe tells us, a camel can serve for "fully fifty years."

Huc points out in his narrative that, oddly enough, the camel has only two defenses against other animals. One is its piercing, prolonged cry, and the other is "its huge shapeless ugly frame, which resembles, at a distance, a heap of ruins." Not to leave out its best defense against man, Huc does describe the "vehement sneeze, wherewith it discharges, from nose and mouth, a mass of filth against the object which it seeks to intimidate or to annoy."

And, as far as man goes, there are other characteristics that to Huc's eyes make the animal one to be avoided. It is awkward, its breath has an "excessive" stench, and it has "hare-lips" and "callosities" on its body. These grievous traits are overcome, however, by its gentleness and docility, not to mention its efficiency and utter servitude to man.

The Bactrian can move on any kind of ground, though it was fitted with sheepskin shoes during Huc's travels when the going was rough. Without shoes the feet of the animal became tender. It would lie down and there were then only two choices: wait for it to get up, or abandon it. It was apparently wise to avoid wet ground, too, where the camel "slips and slides, and generally, after staggering about like a drunken man, falls heavily on its side."

Ordinarily, the camel's coat is in tune with the season it encounters, shedding towards the end of spring, when every last bristle drops before a new coat begins to grow; the animal appears to have been shaved. At this point it is very vulnerable to cold, to dampness, to the wind, and must be protected for a short time until the new growth is long enough. The Bactrian, in its full coat, is different from the Arabian camel in that it seems to think walking in the teeth of a cold north wind is a pleasure.

The wool lost during shedding time may be used for many things, not the least important of which is the rope used for tying the load. Further contributing to man's needs, the milk of the beast is excellent and provides large quantities of butter and cheese. The Tartars did not care for the flesh, Huc tells us, but did use the hump. It was cut into slices and dissolved into tea. Though Huc did not taste it, the Tartars also made a dish of the feet.

Prompted by a removable wooden peg in the nose, the Bactrians were quick to respond to the orders of their masters, but not always without their long, plaintive cries. Yet apparently they were either ready to move at the slightest pull or simply refused to budge at all. When crossing rivers or ice or when their feet were tender, the animals made the most stubborn mule seem eager to please. They could be beaten, pulled, kicked, and still refuse to move. Even during a brush fire on the desert, Abbe Huc says they would not move until their very hair had been singed. "You may pull

their noses, or nearly kill them with blows, yet not
make them advance a step; they would die sooner."

To the dwellers of the desert, the Bactrian's endurance is legend and is an important factor in man's
own survival. Huc claims the camels are able to go a
fortnight or even a month without drinking or eating,
and that they will eat anything, even foods other animals will not touch, such as briars, thorns and tree bark.

How much could the reader in 1850 depend on
Huc's appraisal of the Bactrians? We know one thing
the camel drivers in western America learned on their
own, which was also described by the good Abbe:
"The first portion of our journey . . . was accom-
plished without interruption, sundry anathemas ex-
cepted, which were hurled against us as we ascended
a mountain, by a party of Chinese merchants, whose
mules upon sight of our camels . . . became frightened
and took to their heels at full speed, dragging after
them, and in one or two instances, overturning the
wagons to which they were harnessed." The camels
would continue to scare other animals on sight as they
travelled the trails of the West.

The Dreams of Otto Esche and His Bactrian Camels

When Lt. Edward F. Beale brought a train of twenty-four camels from Camp Verde, Texas, to Fort Tejon, California, where he arrived in November of 1857, newspapers gave frequent accounts of the camels' activities in California and Arizona. "Uncle Sam's Camels," as they were known, were of the one-hump dromedary breed from the Mideast countries.[1] They remained at Fort Tejon for a number of years, and during that time the beasts were used to carry supplies to Fort Mojave and Fort Yuma on the Colorado River and to other communities.

In Texas, under Colonel Robert E. Lee,[2] the army made frequent sojourns from Camp Verde into the mountainous areas of the state with dromedary trains carrying feed and water for the horses and mules only, who could not withstand the heat nor eat the cactus of the desert. The camels could live off the desert. So successful were these trials that Congress was urged by Secretary of War John B. Floyd in 1859 to purchase a thousand camels for military use, but this was to no avail. In 1860 he again made a similar futile recommendation.

---

[1] The United States Army did have one large male Bactrian, which was brought to California.

[2] Lee later went on to become one of the Confederacy's most distinguished Generals.

About this time, bookseller's shelves held E. R. M. Huc's *Travels in Tartary, Thibet, and China, 1844-1846* described in the introduction to this work. He graphically described a Bactrian camel market where he saw that "to the cries of buyers and the sellers who are quarreling or talking, as people talk when a revolt is at its height, are joined the long groans of the poor camels whose noses are incessantly tweaked to try their address in kneeling and rising." Father Huc emphasized the load-carrying ability of these large camels, as well as endurance in cold mountainous regions in China and Tibet, and in the extreme heat of the Mongolian deserts.

In June of 1859, rumors came to San Francisco that prospectors searching the eastern side of the Sierra Nevada had stumbled on some "black rock" specimens that were assayed by a Placerville man and showed a value of $3,000 in silver and $870 in gold per ton of ore. The Comstock Lode came to the lips of hundreds of miners who had previously worked in the Mother Lode on the western slope of the Sierra, and another rush was on.

Not long after this discovery, and with numerous mines going into operation, merchants in San Francisco began to receive orders for huge amounts of salt to be used in the reduction of the silver ore. By coincidence, salt brine was being harvested at the southern end of San Francisco Bay, near San Jose, to supply the needs of local communities. By the spring of 1860, long lines of mules were carrying salt wrapped in burlap sacks through to Placerville and over the high passes to Virginia City, Nevada.

The potential profits in this kind of lucrative business aroused the attention of a man who must have heard about the camels and the demand for salt. He was Otto Esche, a leading German importer and commission merchant in San Francisco who conducted his business at 159 Jackson Street. Esche had been naturalized on August 11, 1856, in San Francisco. When he learned the mines were paying $120 per ton of salt, it did not take him long to calculate the profits from the use of Bactrian camels. It was asserted they could carry over twice the load of a mule, or 1,000 pounds, as compared to 400. Esche quickly decided to go to China and purchase some camels. With a few associates, including M. Frisius, he arranged with Captain Andrew Worth to charter the captain's schooner, the *Caroline E. Foote*. Esche shipped on as a passenger for a voyage to the Orient. The ship's cargo and passengers entered Castris (or Castries) Bay and landed at Nicolaessky, Siberia (now Nikolayevsk, Amur Province, U.S.S.R.), in the early spring of 1860.

Captain Worth had previously made a voyage to this bay when it was an important military and naval base in the Crimean War and a chief commercial port in the northern Pacific trade in 1860. Boats plied regularly between San Francisco and Nicolaessky during the summer.

While Captain Worth stayed with his vessel, Esche hired Asian camel drivers and penetrated into Mongolia, where he bought thirty-two Bactrians in the Amur River country. In driving them through the Mongolian desert to the seaport, he lost seventeen of them from the scarcity of food. The remaining fifteen were hoisted by slings onto the deck of the *Caroline E. Foote,* which departed about the first of June. Captain Worth promised to make a return trip and Esche went back to the Amur country for more camels. As Esche

sought camel sellers, he dreamed that if the outcome
of his enterprise in the mining districts were successful,
he would organize a camel express between San Francisco and Salt Lake City, and another from San Bernardino to El Paso.

The Bactrians on the ship were in very bad condition, and those in charge did not know how to care
for or feed them. The man who was ordered placed
in charge of the beasts was Andrew McFarlan, who
had no experience with livestock of any kind. Under
Captain Worth's guidance, stalls made of poles fastened together with ropes were constructed. A piece
of plank was nailed fore and aft alongside the stalls
and the poles athwart ship were lashed to this. Fine
gravel and some soil were strewn over the floor and
hay spread over it. The stalls were cleaned nearly
every day. With the help of another man, McFarlan
kept a watch on the camels day and night, maintaining
a light to make sure the animals did not become caught
in their halters. The men cleaned and brushed off all
fifteen camels. When the animals laid down, their legs
were taken out from under them and rubbed with
gunny sacks because they were shedding their mangy
coat of hair. This was done every three or four days
throughout the entire fifty-six day passage from Castris
to San Francisco Bay. Captain Worth probably stopped
at Hakodadi (now Hakodate) on Hokkaida Island,
Japan, to take on a fresh supply of food and water for
the longest part of the voyage, which followed the
40°N parallel over 6,000 miles of the Pacific Ocean.

Lashing had been made for the animals but the crew
did not find it necessary to use it because the vessel
encountered only strong breezes, no stormy weather.
McFarlan supplied hay for feed, but it was not more

than one-half allowance of food for the long voyage. The feed was supplemented by barley mixed with oil every third or fourth day, but no more than that in order to avoid killing the animals with too much barley.

On July 25, 1860, the schooner landed at San Francisco with fifteen full-grown camels. They were consigned to M. Frisius and Company. The Bactrians were lean, with their double humps shrivelled down to mere skinny sacks which hung in flabby ugliness over their sides. One of them died four days after arrival and another one about a month later. It had cost Esche $2,250 to charter the ship and $1,100 to freight the camels.

So they could regain their strength, the animals were turned loose on the good pasture near Mission Dolores in San Francisco. As soon as they had recuperated, an attractive announcement advertised that they would be placed on display to raise money for the benefit of the German Benevolent Society of San Francisco. The Bactrians were to be seen in all colors: gray, tawny, yellowish, and even black. The public was informed that under a native camel driver's direction, "These intelligent animals will be made to kneel, rise or move at the word of command, and go through their interesting performances."

The exhibition took place in a large tent erected on the floor of the Music Hall on Bush Street. The camels could be seen from 11 A.M. until 10 P.M. and the show went on for almost two weeks. The price of admission was 50¢ for adults and 25¢ for children. It closed on August 11th.

On September 11th another advertisement appeared in the San Francisco and Los Angeles papers, and possibly as far away as Victoria, British Columbia.

The one which appeared in Los Angeles was placarded throughout town:

By Poulterer, De Ro & Eldridge

Office and Salesroom, Corner California &
Front Streets, San Francisco.
Peremptory Sale
of
Bactrian Camels
Imported from the Amoor River
Ex Caroline E. Foote.
On Wednesday, Oct. 10, 1860
We will Sell at Public Auction
In Lots to Suit Purchasers,
for Cash,
13 Bactrian Camels,

From a cold and mountainous country, comprising 6 males and 7
females, (5 being with young), all in fine health and condition.
* * * For further particulars, inquire of the Auctioneers.

When the day arrived for the sale of the camels, only a small crowd appeared, and only two animals were sold the first day. One of them brought $425 and the other $475. The sale continued the next day, but the bidding was so low the Bactrians were withdrawn from sale. The auctioneers were instructed by the agents to make no sale for under $1,200. Not knowing how to care for them, Mr. Frisius consigned the four males and six females to Julius Bandmann.

For an entire year the ten animals were kept in a pasture on Pacific Street just beyond its intersection with Larkin. The camels grazed the vacant lands and were driven regularly over the sand hills to the Presidio for their favorite food, the thistle. Bandmann studied their habits and dispositions carefully, and tested them at work in various ways. He would load them with as much as 650 pounds of sand each to simulate the load of the salt packs. To test their strength and agility, he drove them over the sand hills and down the steep cliff trails.

Meanwhile, Otto Esche continued to search for more mature and healthy camels and finally collected some sixty animals. He put them in a corral at Nicolaessky to prevent them from straying, and hired two camel drivers, Ali and Assan, as caretakers.

About September 10, 1861, the *Caroline E. Foote* arrived in Nicolaessky for its second round trip. A week later the bark *Dollart* brought in a cargo. She was built at Emden, Hanover, Germany, in 1856, and she had left Germany bound for Newcastle. From London, she went to Melbourne, Australia, and carried cargo between the islands of the Dutch East Indies. She was homeward bound when Captain J. H. C. Muggenborg docked at Nicolaessky.

The arrival of the *Dollart* must have been a great surprise and relief to Esche, for the ship could assist in transporting the many camels he had collected. Esche made arrangements with Captain Muggenborg for exclusive charter of his vessel, a schooner of about 311 tons, some five times larger than the *Caroline E. Foote* at sixty tons. On September 18th Esche signed an agreement in which Muggenborg was to be given $4,500 as freight costs for the cargo of camels, toward which Esche paid $2,500; the remainder was to be paid on arrival in San Francisco. The agreement included passage, fare, and accomodation for Esche and several others. There were eleven men in the crew: five Malays, two Arabs, and four men from Singapore. The German Consul at Nicolaessky certified the conditions of the agreement:

It is this day mutually agreed between Cptn J. H. C.

Müggenborg, Master of the Hanoverian Bark "Dollart," for
and on behalf of himself and Owners of the said Vessel of 311
Tons register, now lying in the Bay of de Castries, and Mr.
Otto Esche, Merchant at Nicolaefsk, that the said Ship being
tight, staunch and strong and every way fitted for the voyage
from Castries Bay via Saugar Strait to San Francisco, California, shall load at Castries Bay a Cargo of Camels and or
other merchandise the Charterer may ship, not exceeding what
she can reasonably stow and carry over and above her tackle,
apparel and provisions from bulkhead to bulkhead, and being
so loaded shall therewith proceed immediately – wind and
weather permitting to San Francisco, Upper California, via
the Strait of Saugar to refresh and to take food, water and
provisions at Hokodadi if necessary; and on delivery of the
cargo according to the bills of lading signed by the Captain
shall receive freight for the whole cargo the sum of Four
thousand, five hundred Dollars U.S. Currency in full; of this
freight money Two thousand Rubles to be prepaid before the
sailing of the vessel from Castries Bay in gold coin or Russian
money at Charterers option – the Ruble for seventy five cents
American currency; and the remainder in Cash before delivery
of the Cargo at San Francisco. For loading and discharging
thirty five lay days are allowed . . . The Vessel to haul at
San Francisco so near as she can safely get to any wharf or
place required by Charterer, the half of the Wharfage and of
all inward expenses to be paid by Charterer. The Ship's water-
casks and tanks so far as they are not wanted for by the Crew
to be for the use of the Camels, other means for carrying water
to be furnished by Charterer, as well as the materials for con-
structing proper stalls for the Camels, this work to be done
by the vessel.

The Cargo to be received and delivered at Ship's tackles.
Three passengers to have free passage in the Cabin with regular Cabin fare for Three hundred Rubles in full, and no other
passengers to be taken without consent of Charterer.

The Captain to pay three per cent for insurance of the
amount of freight money to be paid before the sailing from
de Castries.

The Ship to be consigned, at the port of discharging to
Charterer or Agent free of Commission under this Charter.

Penalty for non-performance of the Charter Five thousand dollars.

And for the true performance of all of the above stipulations and agreements both parties have hereunto set their hands at Nicolaesk of Amoor, this 6th/18th day of September 1861.

The Cargo to be delivered and taken from alongside the Ship at Charterers risk.

J. H. C. MUGGENBORG
OTTO ESCHE

Witness:
GUSTAV BRODROSER

Stalls were made under the direction of Captain Worth, with the help of Jesse S. Hall, the mate, and Seaman Charles Landes, who constructed them. Otto Esche put a lot of lumber on board, along with 100 pounds of nails, and gave instructions to build twenty-five stalls. There must have been some change in plans because when Captain Worth and the *Caroline E. Foote* sailed out of the port on October 12th, there were only ten Bactrians aboard his ship as compared to fifteen the first trip. But when the *Dollart* sailed she carried forty-four camels leaving a shortage of some twenty stalls. The animals were loaded carefully with the help of the Russians.

Captain Muggenborg was apparently not a considerate man when it came to bedding down his cargo of Bactrians in safety. Nor did it appear that Otto Esche gave it much personal attention, going into the hold only every two or three days to inspect the animals and stalls. Both Muggenborg and Esche had been warned by Captain Worth about excessive feeding with barley because it tended to bloat the animals if used continuously.

The *Dollart* left Nicolaessky on October 21st but laid in Castris Bay until the 25th, for which no explanation was made. During this time, efforts were made to get carpenters to build more stalls, but they refused to work among the camels. The lack of stalls caused the animals to be thrown against each other and bruised. One night nearly all camels quartered on the starboard side were over on the port side, and one was found dead.

Finally, the *Dollart* sailed for Hakodadi, Japan, some 800 miles away, and arrived there in twelve days, during which time six camels died. One of the small animals was hanged by the halter of a larger one.

The hold was not cleansed during the entire trip, and the camels were not groomed, rubbed, or cleaned. Jesse S. Hall, the mate, with the help of Ali and Assan, looked after them and stayed in the hold to feed and water them. But the captain said Hall's duty was on deck because of several days of rough weather, and the animals were left with insufficient care and stalls to prevent them from falling and banging into each other.

When the *Dollart* arrived at Hakodadi on November 5th, Esche immediately went to see the American Consul about the failure of the captain to carry out the terms of the Charter Party.

Esche met with C. A. Fletcher, Acting Consul of the United States in Hakodadi, and entered a note of protest on November 6 against the *Dollart* and her captain. Fletcher then directed Fred Wilkie and Thomas S. Stephenson to survey the *Dollart* and report their findings. Their report included the following condemnation of conditions on the boat:

> The stalls made for the Camels [are found] to be totally insufficient for the proper transportation of the animals. We recommend therefore proper Stalls to be built; Judging from what we . . . saw last year on board the Caroline E. Foot . . .

The report of the surveyors was certified by Fletcher and the documents were held by Esche.

After this inspection the schooner was detained, new stalls added, and improvements made on the original ones, but the work was delayed again by carpenters who did not want to work among the camels. Fresh hay was scattered over the rough gravel on the floor, and in some places poles were laid over the ballast to smooth the surface. Still the holds had not been cleaned when the *Dollart* left on November 18th, and they were not to be cleaned until about January 1st. The death of the first camel after leaving Hakodadi was on November 24th, and the last one occurred January 18th, for a total of seventeen Bactrians lost.

During one part of the voyage Esche fell down a hatchway off a passageway near the captain's stateroom, which was used by passengers. The hatchway opened on the stern of the ship, a very unusual place to have it. It was 4½ feet wide and slightly longer. Since it was badly lighted, a fall was not unexpected, even on an afternoon of fine weather, when Esche fell. He yelled for help and had to be carried to his stateroom. A lady passenger, Mrs. Herman Muller, and some of the crew had the same experience but were not severely hurt.

After seventy days at sea with several very stormy days, the *Dollart* finally docked at San Francisco on January 26, 1862, with only twenty Bactrians alive. They were placed under the care of Julius Bandmann.

That evening Esche went to see a Doctor Regensberger, who found the sixth rib on his right side broken, with contusions of the short ribs, which irritated the pleura causing great pain in breathing, and coughing.

The next day Esche entered suit for $7,300 against the schooner and her master, Captain Muggenborg, for the loss of his camels. The case was brought to trial before Judge Ogden Hoffman in United States District Court. Hall McAllister, an outstanding attorney in the San Francisco of his day, was the lawyer for Esche, and J. B. Manchester represented Muggenborg. The evidence presented to the court left no doubt that the *Dollart* was not seaworthy when she left Castris Bay, and that the camels had been neglected and inhumanely treated. Esche was awarded damages to the amount of $6,240, or $260 for each camel lost. In his decision, Judge Hoffman said, "It is impossible to read the proofs without the conviction that gross neglect, and even inhumanity, had been practiced by some one towards these unhappy beasts. It is not pretended that any disease prevailed among them. Their supply of food, at least from Hakodadi to this port, was abundant. They were in good condition when shipped. The voyage, though long, was not extraordinarily tempestuous." [3]

Esche also sued the *Dollart* and Muggenborg for violation of the contract made when the ship was chartered. Among his claims was one for $4,000 for the injury he received falling down the hatchway. The total damages asked by Esche, including the loss of the camels, were $15,375.

After being repaired, the *Dollart* was possessed by the United States Marshal, William Rabe, and sold on March 31st with her furniture and full equipment for $6,500. After all the claims were settled by the court, Esche was awarded $6,240 with court costs of $187.50.

Long before the *Dollart* arrived, the *Caroline E. Foote* had docked at the San Francisco wharf on November 15, 1861, with ten healthy camels which were

---

[3] Judge Ogden Hoffman, *Esche vs. Muggenborg*, U.S. District Court, San Francisco, California, March 29, 1862.

delivered to Bandmann. Captain Worth later testified at the court hearing for Esche's claim about his contact with Muggenborg at Nicolaessky and his warning about how to care for the animals.

Bandmann decided before Captain Worth and Esche returned that the Bactrians from the first shipment were strong and healthy enough to be put to work hauling salt to the Nevada silver mines. It is possible someone proposed to purchase the group when they arrived in Virginia City.

During the course of exercising his charges, Bandmann must have encountered difficulties when mules and horses caught sight of the ungainly and odorous beasts, and scattered far and wide to avoid them. This was one problem Father Huc had mentioned. Bandmann must have begun to wonder about mules and horses scattering in the sandy valleys around San Francisco. What sort of reception would he get going over the narrow roads and trails of the Sierra? He had been over those trails carrying merchandise to Nevada towns, both by horseback and by wagon. He had found that a wagon could cause a blockade in narrow parts of the trails.

At that time, there were three possible way to cross the Sierra. The only wagon road was from Hangtown (Placerville),[4] with winding, steep up-and-down grades, and very rocky, almost treeless, terrain, which gave no help in warding off the heat of the sun. It went over Echo Summit at a steep pass of about 7,400 feet in elevation, after which there was an almost perpendicular drop down to Lake Tahoe through Daggett Pass at 7,440 feet, and into Genoa and Carson City, a distance of 100 miles. This was considered the worst

---

[4] Named Placerville in 1850 (nicknamed Hangtown in 1849).

passage, with heavy wagons and trains of mules and horses crowding the narrow, mostly one-way road, where it was extremely dangerous to pass either way.

The second route, called the Big Tree route because it is surrounded by the Calaveras Big Trees, was out of Angels Camp. It had an easy grade and was relatively straight to Bear Valley. Then the steep, winding, narrow trail to Ebbetts Pass began. Completed in 1856 by Major John Ebbetts for use by the military, the trail reached the summit at 8,730 feet. It then dropped steeply into Hope Valley where the Carson River rushed through, and on to Woodford, Genoa, and Carson City, a total distance of 120 miles. The traffic was light, and consisted only of mule and horse trains. The heavily forested trail was considered 20° cooler than the other open passes.

The third route was the Sonora Pass trail which began at Sonora. It was not too steep nor winding until it reached the Dardanelle River. Then the climb up the steeply winding trail began over granite boulders to Sonora Pass at 9,600 feet. A steep drop of over 3,000 feet followed, down into Fales Hot Springs. After this first 100 miles, the trail turned north for seventy miles over the desert to Carson City. Although the traffic was not heavy, the trail over Sonora Pass tried the patience of the horse and mule drivers and tourists alike. It was the longest route to the mines, and the open trail was very hot to travel in the summer.

A group of tourists from San Francisco took the Sonora Pass going and returned by the Big Trees trail. One member of the group had this to say:

> The next day we passed the Carson Canon, and taking the Big Tree road, we camped that night one mile to the west of the Summit. The road thus far from the canon far exceeded in excellence all that we had previously anticipated of

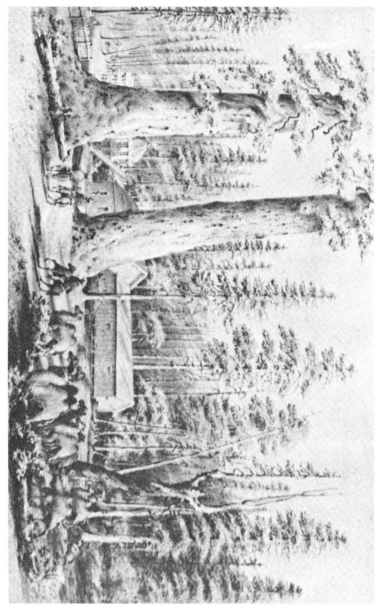

CAMELS AT MAMMOTH GROVE
This sketch by Edward Vischer shows the camels enroute
to the Washoe Mines by the Big Tree Route.
Courtesy, Francis P. Farquhar.

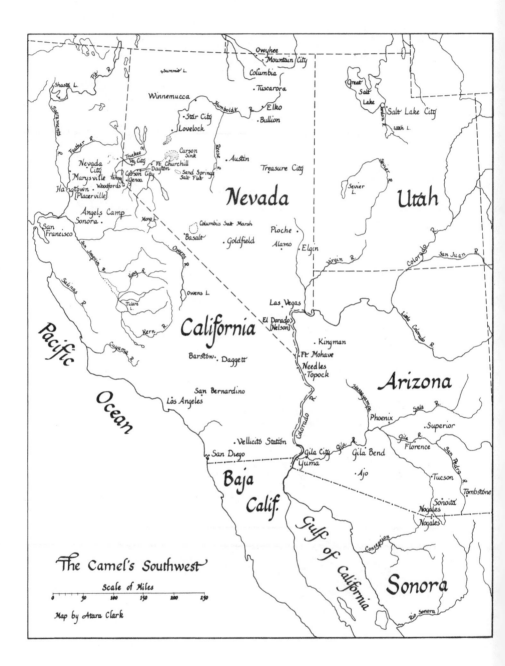

The Camel's Southwest

Scale of Miles

0   50   100   150   200   250

Map by Atara Clark

it, presenting a strange contrast with that over which we passed on our outward journey, and which, we will venture to assert, will hold true also in regard to any other road over the Sierra Nevadas, and we predict that when its superior excellence is more generally known, almost the entire over land emigration to our State will pass over this road. One of our companions who had twice passed over both the Placerville and Big Tree roads, and mixed up as we were with the emigrants, gave essentially the same conclusion.[5]

In September of 1861, Bandmann decided to take the Big Tree route as shown by a sketch made by Edward Vischer, who was already at the Calaveras Big Trees area, known then as Mammoth Grove.[6] A spacious park surrounded a large hotel and other buildings. A pavilion, erected on a flat stump some twenty-five feet in diameter, was used as a dancing platform, and there was a farm to supply food for the way-worn emigrants, pleasure parties, and visitors from around the world. All this was surrounded by the magnificent grove of trees, which grew to a height of 300 feet.

Vischer had been making numerous sketches of these scenes for several weeks when Bandmann and his camels appeared around the bend. About this one sketch there are three interesting features: 1) The camels were not saddled with freight or goods; 2) They were led by three men, two ahead and one following, but other sketches showed two men closing in the rear; 3) The animals were not tied together by a rope leading from the nose ring of each animal, as is the custom in the Orient.

The first observation is interesting because it may tell us that Bandmann had decided not to overload the animals while they were crossing the high passes, where

[5] *Hutchings' California Magazine,* Nov., 1860, p. 307.

[6] Francis P. Farquhar, "Camels in the Sketches of Edward Vischer," Calif. Hist. Soc. Qtly., Vol. IX, No. 4 (Dec., 1930), pp. 332-35.

they might risk an accident. Secondly, the single man at the rear was probably Bandmann, who had taken so much interest in the animals and wished to make sure of their safe delivery to Virginia City. The two men ahead are intriguing. Were they the Chevalier brothers of Dayton, Nevada? Their name is frequently mentioned in the annals of the camel episode. Or were they the two Americans, Adam Heffley and Henry Ingram, who had been sent by a syndicate in British Columbia to get information on the animals? Lastly, the absence of a line holding the camels together in a long train may have indicated that Bandmann was unaware of the tie-rope system used in the Orient. This system was later found to be an important factor in preventing the Bactrians from stampeding under startling circumstances.

Vischer made another sketch of the Mammoth Grove and the camels before they proceeded to Holden Station, Hermit Valley, some thirty miles east. He sketched the log cabins and the Bactrians basking in the sun while people were waiting for the passing of the Pony Express. At the moment of the sketch, an immigrant train was passing on its way to California. The mules in the train became frightened at the sight and the smell of the camels and started to run away, all of which is recorded by the artist.

Ten miles farther on, the camel train passed through Ebbetts Pass, where Vischer made a very fine sketch of the mountain peaks and passing Bactrians. The next sketch was of Summit Lake, showing "the grandeur of this solitary wilderness where the camels grazed on the rich sward of the near shore." [7] Here they turned north toward Woodford, passing the Carson River.

Vischer's last sketch on this trip was the encampment

---

[7] *Ibid.*

overlooking Carson Valley. He noted that "on a halt, though fatigued from a day's journey, they [the camels] like to climb an eminence near the camp, to obtain a more extensive view, then quietly kneel down, as though in contemplation." [8] He also noted the camels' aversion to, and apparent impatience toward strangers. "Though usually slow in their movements, their attitudes were constantly changing, rendering it difficult to sketch these animals in nature." [9] While Vischer was sketching them, he was suddenly annoyed by the appearance of "the snouts of five animals that appeared so absorbed in their meal, [that] by rubbing against our paper, [they] put an effective protest against all further portraiture." [10] This sketch still showed three men sitting on the ground before several tents, looking at the far distant scene of Carson Valley.

It is apparent that Vischer followed the caravan across the Sierra and on to Virginia City, where the nine Bactrians [11] were sold for an unrecorded price, but probably around $250 each to defray the cost of Captain Worth's shipping charges, which averaged out to about this figure.

Shortly thereafter, Bandmann and his associates took the trail southeast to the Columbus Salt Marsh, which was not far from the fork of the Walker River, and a distance of 150 miles from Virginia City. For the first time camel trains carried salt to this country. The load was held to about 500 pounds at first because of the rough country and high mountain trails. On the return to Virginia City, the mill paid the customary rate of $120 per ton, which amounted to a profit of about $265 for the trip. Since the Bactrians lived off

[8] *Ibid.*   [9] *Ibid.*   [10] *Ibid.*

[11] Three shipments of camels, totalling 45 animals, arrived in San Francisco. Only nine went with Bandmann to Nevada.

the desert plants and drank from pools of desert water, Bandmann's group made a clear profit of about $250 after deducting the cost of their own food and supplies. The animals moved at the speed of about thirty miles per day, so the round trip took about ten days.

It had been a long hot drive over the dreary desert, full of very exhausting work walking the camels over the sandy soil. Presumably Bandmann soon realized the pay was ridiculously low at about $8 per day per man. A miner could do better than that and still be at home. If the transportation of salt were to be profitable, the services of white drivers would have to be substituted by Arabs or Mexicans at a lower rate of pay, and this eventually proved to be the case. We may assume that Heffley and Ingram returned to Victoria, British Columbia, later in October to report their experiences to the syndicate mentioned in the following paragraphs.

Bandmann returned to San Francisco where he was soon confronted by the ten camels brought in by Captain Worth on his second voyage. The captain informed Bandmann that Esche was returning with another load of Bactrians on the bark *Dollart*. By the end of January, 1862, Esche came with twenty camels in tow and asked Bandmann to keep all thirty animals in corrals until he could find a buyer.

With the help of the Arabs, Assan and Ali, and with the advice of Captain Worth, Bandmann set to work to clean and rub the camels down with oil, and to feed the sick ones with corn meal and hot water, poured down from a bottle. The animals were placed in clean stalls, fed and watered twice a day, and several times a week they were exercised in the valleys.

Esche was a very sick and disappointed man with heavy losses from his ventures. When Bandmann sold the nine camels in Nevada, and gave him $2,000 minus ten percent commission, the poor fellow was grateful.

Around the first of April, Esche was visited by John C. Callbreath of Victoria, British Columbia, who inquired into the usefulness of the Bactrians and wished to see them at work. Callbreath represented a syndicate headed by Frank Laumeister, a merchant of Victoria and a former miner who had followed the gold rush to the Fraser River in 1858, and up into the wild Cariboo country.[12] Callbreath was possibly accompanied by Henry Ingram and Adam Heffley to help select the animals.

Callbreath came to see if Esche's Bactrians were available and was surprised to learn that 45 of them had reached San Francisco in three shipments from the Orient; nine of them had been sent into Nevada. Since then some of them had died or been sold to individuals, leaving about thirty camels in a local corral. Perhaps with the help of Ingram and Heffley, Callbreath selected twenty-three of them, leaving seven of the animals, probably too young or too sick or too aged for the trip to Victoria. Callbreath paid $6,000 to Bandmann. When the camels were ready to be shipped, one died and was replaced. Consequently, when the stern-wheel steamer *Herman* left in April of 1862, twenty-three camels were on board, bound for Esquimault, near Victoria, with George S. Wright as captain. Ali and Assan, who had cared for the camels, accompanied the *Herman*. They were to receive $12 per month, the customary fee for camel drivers.

We may now sum up the financial status of Esche. It has been noted that the total damage he claimed was

---

[12] Other Syndicate members involved in camel speculation included: Frank Laumeister, George Steity, Gus Hoffmeister, old man Neufeldon, Charles Gowan and John Kingham.

$15,373. On the credit side, he had been awarded
$6,240, plus $187, or $6,427 by the court; a judgment
against Muggenborg for $500, paid; $2,000 from
Bandmann; and $6,000 from Callbreath, making a
total compensation of about $14,927 or within $448
of the losses he claimed. So far so good.

But Esche was out the $6,750 paid Captain Worth
for his two voyages. It is recorded that Esche purchased eighty-six camels, but it is quite possible that
he brought more than that back with him, up to ninety
animals.[13] If we are to be governed by the prices paid
in the Levant during the Crimean War, the prices
ranged from $40 to $50 for the best females, and from
$75 to $100 for the best males. Esche's expeditures
may have averaged around $50 for camels of both
sexes, as a minimum in Asia, or a total of $4,500. One
cannot but wonder how Esche managed to pay out such
large sums of money in a strange and hostile country.
We might consider the difficulties encountered by the
United States purchasing commission, headed by Major
Henry Wayne in the Levant in 1855. The United States
had good diplomatic relations with these countries, yet
it took Wayne two and a half months in the Levant
before he finally got thirty-three dromedaries on board
a supply vessel. We can only imagine the circumstances
by which Esche, a private citizen, managed to purchase his Bactrians.

We have no knowledge of the people who may have
accompanied Esche across the rugged Amur country
into the Mongolian desert, a distance of 600 to 800
miles. Nor do we know of the market places where the
animals were sold, the language barriers or the cus-
toms. Certainly Esche never saw a Bactrian before in

---

[13] Nearly half of the camels were lost, due to the severity of the voyage
from Nicolaessky to San Francisco.

his life, with his only knowledge being what he learned of their habits from Father Huc's book. Nor do we know the intracacies of foreign money exchange, or whether it was solved with the help of the German consul, Gustav Brodroser, at Nicolaessky.

We have already estimated Esche's payment of $6,750 to Captain Worth and approximately $4,500 to camel dealers in the Orient, for a total of $11,250 not accounted for in his lawsuits. Obviously we know nothing of his dealings with the Asiatic camel sellers, who may have played tricks similar to the ones Major Wayne encountered, including the sale of poorly fed, diseased and weak camels at high prices. Esche lost seventeen out of thirty-two Bactrians on his first purchasing expedition.

This is the last ever heard of Esche, Bandmann, Captains Worth and Muggenborg, and of their vessels. This chapter on the procurement of the Bactrians in the Orient is closed, and we look forward to a new life for these unfortunate Islamic animals who seem to kneel and pray to Allah.

2

Frank Laumeister's Bactrians in the Cariboo Gold Country

There is good reason to believe that Frank Laumeister, head of a British Columbia syndicate, must have seen an advertisement of a camel sale in the Victoria newspaper (the *British Colonist*) on September 11, 1860. The ad probably gave him the idea of using camels to pack supplies into the recently discovered gold mines of British Columbia Cariboo Country. Laumeister had seen the almost insuperable difficulties the early pioneers experienced before the construction of the Cariboo dirt roads packing everything on their backs.

Laumeister was reasonably convinced that an animal capable of doing the work of two mules, of traveling thirty miles a day, of being able to live on sagebrush and not needing water for seven days, and of thriving in hot and cold climates would be a valuable asset to any pack train.

In the beginning, packing by mule up the Fraser River was very profitable. In early 1861 the shipping rate from Yale to Quesnel Forks, a distance of 300 miles, was one dollar a pound. But as more packers entered the trade, prices soon dropped to 50¢ a pound. Since the Bactrian could carry far more than the mules, the profits could be astronomical. It did not take Frank Laumeister long to calculate the opportunities offered by the camels. He was well known in Victoria, a very

likable and trustworthy person, so when he called
together a group of his friends, many responded.

The story of how the camel enterprise was promoted
was told by Agnes E. Tate in the *Daily Colonist,* Victoria, British Columbia, on October 6, 1957.

A CAMEL SPAT ON MR. GOWAN

It was the year 1861, in Victoria, the capital of the Crown
Colony of Vancouver Island. The Cariboo gold rush was in
full swing. A group of businessmen who had decided there
was more money to be made out of the gold-seekers than in
seeking gold for themselves, were discussing what they hoped
would be a new means of making money. They were sitting
in the New England Cafe, owned and operated by the three
of them, and for nearly one hundred years afterwards, known
as one of the finest eating places on the Pacific Coast.

"But I tell you they've been using them in the California
gold field," said Frank Laumeister, "and the U.S. Army has
been using them since 1858. You freighted stuff yourself in
the California gold rush, didn't you Charlie, and made good
money out of it, too?"

"Yes," said Charlie Gowan doubtfully, "but that was with
horses and mules. These camels, now – I don't know. I sailed
between Bombay and Port Said when I was a boy and I saw
lots of camels but a fellow had to know how to handle them.
These camels from Manchuria are different, and maybe we
could find men who could handle them and maybe we
couldn't."

Ach, come on Charlie," cried Gus Hoffmeister. "You're
usually ready to take a chance. These camels can travel twice
as far in a day as a packhorse, and carry a much bigger load.
I tell you, you come in on this deal with us, and you name
your next baby after me and I leave him all my money."

"But supposing she's a girl?" asked Charlie.

"Then name her in memory of Frank's wife," said Gus,
who was a bachelor, "and I still leave her my money. Ach!
poor Frank. Sad for his wife to die so young. Only 36. And
left him with five girls to care for."

And so it was agreed. An agent was sent to San Francisco
to confer with Otto Esche.

The party contracted a deal with Esche, and the ship carrying the camels docked in Victoria on the morning of April 14, 1862. The new owners went down to examine their property. One of the camels, evidently disgusted with its travels, spat, as camels will, right in Charlie Gowan's eye, and the usually good-natured man was furious.

The new arrivals caused great excitement among the white citizens and a tremendous waugh-waughing among the Indians when the strange two-humped creatures were seen coming ashore after the more usual cargo of horses, mules, cows, pigs, and sheep had been discharged.

Agnes Tate gives additional information:

CARIBOO CAMELS

In his article in *British Columbia Magazine* about Lillooet, Bruce Ramsey again mentions the Cariboo camels. Seeing that so many names have been mentioned at different times in connection with their importation I thought your readers might be interested in the following notations made by my grandfather, Charles Gowan, in 1884:

"In 1862, Frank Laumeister, George Steity, Gus Hoffmeister, old man Neufelden, John Kingham and myself went into that blessed camel speculation. Every one that was there then knows what profit they were to us!"

I don't think anyone knows for certain who instigated the plan. Both my grandfather and Frank Laumeister were '49ers in California and could have heard of the camels being used there for freight carriers across the desert.

I imagine these men put up the money and other men mentioned were the purchasing agents and the men who did the actual freighting."

We may follow the early progress of the Bactrians as reported in British Columbia newspapers of the day. First, the *Victoria Colonist,* April 15, 1862:

The camels have come. Mr. Colbreath's twenty-three Bactrian Camels arrived in the *Hermann* yesterday. They are singular looking animals, and when driven from the steamer frightened the horses at *Esquimalt* [sic] out of their propriety and a week's appetite. The camels are just now engaged in shedding the winter's coat of hair and present a very scaly appearance. Each has two humps on the back and will pack from 500 to 600 pounds. A practical test of their availability as pack animals in British Columbia will be made in a few days. The Strangers who are guarded by a live Turk, are at Half-Way House.

When the steamer *Hermann* was unloading cargo at Esquimault, a shipping point a few miles west of Victoria, Laumeister was probably in charge since he is most frequently mentioned in the uproar which followed. The report above is the first we have about the appearance of a Bactrian after shedding its heavy coat of winter hair.

The *British Colonist* of Victoria followed the progress:

Friday, May 2, 1862. THE CAMELS were brought to town yesterday and are herded in the lot at the corner of Douglas and Johnson Street.

Tuesday, May 6, 1862. THE CAMELS – Yesterday morning twenty-two of the camels were forwarded by the [steamer] Enterprise to New Westminster. They will be passed over the Harrison-Lillooet trail to Lillooet and from thence will start with the first load for Cariboo as soon as the trail is passable. A great diversity of opinion exists as to the adaptability of these animals for packing purposes in British Columbia, and the failure of a number who were tried in Washoe last year is quoted as a proof of the inability to stand the climate or to traverse rugged mountain passes. The nonsuccess of those tried at Washoe we are assured was owing to the alkali, which abounds in that section rendering their feet sore, and not from the effects of the climate or the rugged character of the trails. The species are known as the Bactrian or two-humped camel, and possess most of the characteristics of the Arabian or one-humped dromedary. They came from the Amoor River where they were used as pack animals, and answered well. Whether they will answer the same purpose in the sister colony is an open question which can only be decided after a fair trial. The dam and her calf have been left behind until strong enough to withstand the fatigue of a journey.

May 24, 1862. THE CAMELS: These animals are to be sent above to Lillooet Flat shortly to pack provisions, etc. on the new line of road. The heaviest load yet placed upon anyone of them is about 350 pounds, but it is supposed that when in good trim each animal will pack nearly double that weight.

May 26, 1862. THE CAMELS have been turned out on Pemberton Meadows for a few days to recruit.

Wednesday, May 28. ARRIVAL OF THE ENTERPRISE: The steamer *Enterprise,* Captain Mouat, arrived from New Westminster at an early hour yesterday morning, with a small express and a half-a-dozen passengers. Very few men remain at Lillooct and supplies are now going forward to the mines with regularity and in considerable quantity. Several pack trains have left Lillooet for Cariboo. The camels have crossed the Brigade trail over which they will be packed with provisions to Cariboo. So far they have proved a success.

Wednesday, June 4. The steamer *Enterprise* arrived from New Westminster yesterday afternoon with 15 passengers and a small amount of treasure. No later news has been received from Cariboo, and no miners are as yet reported on their way down. Stocks of provisions at Lillooet and Lytton are accumulating, business is brisk. The wagon-road on the second portage, Harrison-Lillooet trail, is nearly completed and laden wagons are passing over it. Nine of the camels are packing from Seaton Lake to Lillooet Flat; the remainder are at Bridge River.

Thursday, July 10. The new trail from the mouth of Quesnelle to Lightning Creek is finished, and the camels, several trains of mules, sheep, cattle and horses, have been driven over it.

Newspapers all along the Fraser River were also re-

porting the progress of the camels. One of these was
the *British Columbia* of New Westminster.

Wednesday, May 7, 1862. CAMELS, 21 in number, arrived
by the steamer *Enterprise* on Monday, and went up to Douglas
yesterday on the barge, in tow of the Flying Dutchman. Their
appearance on the Wharf caused great wonder and a "hy-you
waw-waw" amongst the Indians who seemed in great per-
plexity to understand the precise nature of the extraordinary
looking animals.

Saturday, May 17. NEWS FROM ABOVE. The camels are
employed in packing over the Pemberton portage, and are
found to answer admirably. Large quantities of goods are now
passing over the route – more than any previous period.

Saturday, May 24. The Camels are still employed in packing
over Pemberton portage. Altho' we believe these animals do
not quite come up to the expectations of their owners yet
they answer very well, and we have understood an advance
of $600 has been tendered for them. While they carry from
500 to 600 lbs., at a load, being double that of a mule, their
keep costs little or nothing as they pick up all they require by
the way side, no small consideration when feed is 6 to 7 cents
per pound.

Saturday, July 5. INFORMATION OF ANIMALS: We are
indebted to the politeness of the Collector for the following
statement of animals imported into the colony during the
months of April, May and June, which will be interesting
to our readers:
Horses and mules, 3,434; Oxen, 162; Asses, 1; Camels, 21;
Beef Cattle, 1,139; Sheep, 638; Bulls, 9; Cows, 280; Calves,
44; Hogs, 26; Total, 5,754.

The man most responsible for putting the camels in
the news, Francis William Laumeister, was born in
Memlinger, Bavaria, in 1822. He became a naturalized citizen of the United States at Richmond, Virginia, in 1844, and married Agnes Neidt there. The
couple's first child, Agnes Caroline, was born in 1848.
In that same year, Frank Laumeister must have

joined a group bound for Texas, taking a packet ship from New York City to Port Lavaca, on Matagorda Bay.[1] The overland journey to the West began at Port Lavaca. Many who started the trip must have been disheartened by the fear of Indians, cholera, poverty, and the 2,000 miles of wilderness ahead of them. Gold had not yet been discovered in California, but nevertheless many undertook the trek.

Laumeister's party would take the trail through San Antonio to El Paso, 100 days and 673 miles. They would pass through treacherous mountains and the territories of many Indian tribes on their way to Tucson, then continue northwest to the junction of the Salt and Gila rivers. When they met the Colorado River due west, they were three months out of El Paso.

Laumeister crossed the Colorado at the Lower Crossing, about fourteen miles below the Gila-Colorado junction, at the point where the immigrant and military roads left the river. Here the Colorado was about 400 yards wide and running perhaps two miles-per-hour. The banks were lined with willow, cane, and some cottonwood trees, in which Indian huts were concealed. The town of Yuma had yet to be built some years later.

Apparently Laumeister was not a good swimmer, especially where the river was turbulent. He hired "Chief Pasqual of the Cocopah Indians, who swam the river with the rope of Mr. L's mule in his mouth,

---

[1] Port Lavaca was one of the most active and important Texas seaports. Nearby, on an arm of Matagorda Bay, the port of Carlshafen was founded by Carl Zu Solms-Braunfels in 1844. It was to be used as a port of entry by German immigrants. In 1846 it was swept by cholera, and the dead laid unburied in the streets, but it survived in the booming market when the Mexican War ended in 1847. The port soon was known as Indianola, which does not exist today. This is the port where Lt. David Porter landed his army camels. Port Lavaca is on Lavaca Bay. A gulf storm ended the career of Indianola in 1875. It was never rebuilt.

while Mr. L. hung on to the mule's tail and thus succeeded in crossing the river."[2] For this help Laumeister was charged two dollars, and no doubt would have drowned were it not for the Indian's exertion.

Laumeister continued on to Los Angeles, where he started a bakery. He later joined in the gold rush to Mariposa County in 1850 and set up a grocery store at Agua Frio. On February 2, 1851, Laumeister joined the Mariposa Battalion, formed to protect miners and settlers from the Mariposa Indians, who were trying to eject the white man from their lands. Laumeister became Quartermaster and Commissary Officer before the battalion was disbanded on July 1, 1851. During his period of service, the battalion made an expedition against the Yo Semite Indians, and it was probably then that Laumeister became one of the first white men to see Yosemite Valley, as he claimed.

"Dutch Frank," as Laumeister was sometimes nicknamed, apparently continued in the grocery business until 1853, when he was appointed the first flour inspector in San Francisco by California Governor John Bigler. Laumeister held the office for four years, and was also, for a brief time, a member of the Vigilance Committee. He was not to stay in San Francisco much longer.

In 1858 word reached San Francisco that gold had been discovered on the Fraser River in British Columbia. Specimens of the ore had been brought to the Hudson's Bay Company in early 1852, and by February of 1858, the company had 800 ounces of gold in its safe. Art Downs describes the situation and the beginning of the rush in *Wagon Road North.*[3]

---

[2] Frank Laumeister, *Arizona Sentinel,* Yuma City.

[3] Art Downs, *Wagon Road North,* Northwest Digest Ltd., Quesnel, B.C. (July, 1960).

FORT YUMA ON THE COLORADO RIVER
Fort Yuma, overlooking the Colorado River, was drawn
by the Mexican boundary commissioner John R. Bartlett.
From Bartlett, Personal Narrative, Vol. I, 1854.

YUMA CROSSING
This painting by H. B. Mollhouser, Lt. Amiel Whipple's artist, shows
expedition members crossing the Colorado near a Mohave Indian Village, 1853.

FRANK LAUMEISTER
Frank Laumeister at age 37, a photo
taken at San Francisco in 1859.
Courtesy, Provincial Archives, Victoria, B.C.

A BACTRIAN CAMEL IN BRITISH COLUMBIA
This photo of one of the descendants of the camels used to freight
supplies in the Cariboo Country was taken in 1888 at the back of the
Ingram estate. W. H. Smith holds the rope, A. M. McPhail enjoys the ride.
Courtesy, Provincial Archives, Victoria, B.C.

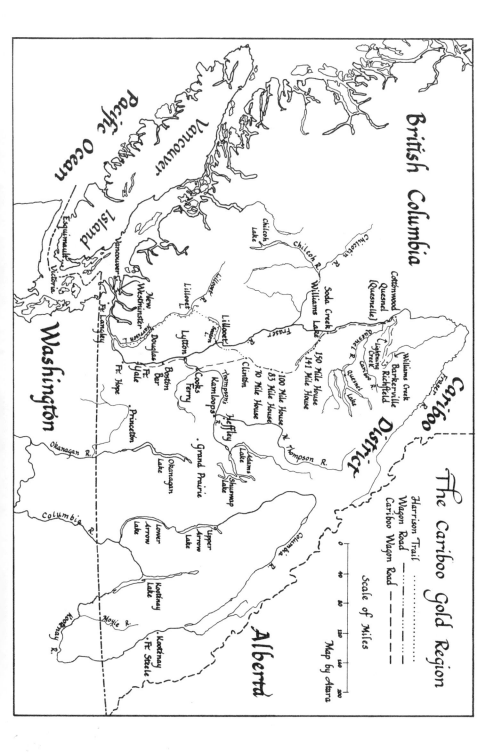

The Cariboo Gold Region

Harrison Trail ·············
Wagon Road ————
Cariboo Wagon Road — — —

Scale of Miles

0   40   80   120   160   200

Map by Atara

British Columbia

Cariboo District

Washington

Alberta

Pacific Ocean

Vancouver Island

Esquimault
Victoria
Ft. Langley
New Westminster
Vancouver I.
Harrison L.
Ft. Hope
Princeton
Ft. Yale
Boston Bar
Cooks Ferry
Lytton
Douglas
Lillooet L.
Lillooet
Lillooet R.
Seton L.
Anderson L.
Chilcoh Lake
Chilcoh R.
Chilcotin R.
Cottonwood
Quesnel (Quesnelle)
Williams Lake
Soda Creek
Williams Creek
Barkerville
Richfield
Lightning Creek
Quesnel R.
Cariboo R.
Quesnel Lake
Fraser R.
150 Mile House
141 Mile House
100 Mile House
83 Mile House
70 Mile House
Clinton
Kamloops
Thompson R.
Jeffrey R.
Adams Lake
Shuswap Lake
Grand Prairie
Okanagan Lake
Okanagan R.
Upper Arrow Lake
Lower Arrow Lake
Columbia R.
Kootenay Lake
Moyie R.
Kootenay R.
Kootenay
Ft. Steele
N. Thompson R.
Fraser R.
Columbia R.

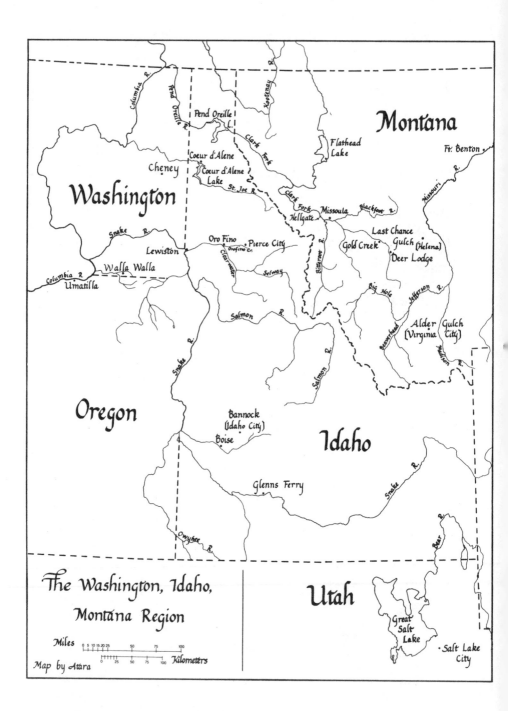

Columbia R.

Pend Oreille R.

Pend Oreille L.

Clark Fork

Kootenay R.

Flathead Lake

Montana

Ft. Benton

Missouri R.

Coeur d'Alene

Cheney

Coeur d'Alene Lake

St. Joe R.

Washington

Clark Fork

Hellgate

Missoula

Blackfoot R.

Snake R.

Oro Fino

Orofino Cr.

Pierce City

Last Chance Gulch (Helena)

Gold Creek

Deer Lodge

Lewiston

Clearwater

Bitterroot R.

Walla Walla

Selway

Columbia R.

Umatilla

Salmon R.

Big Hole

Jefferson R.

Alder Gulch (Virginia City)

Madison R.

Snake R.

Oregon

Salmon R.

Bannock (Idaho City)

Boise

Idaho

Beaverhead R.

Glenns Ferry

Snake R.

Bear R.

Owyhee R.

Utah

The Washington, Idaho, Montana Region

Great Salt Lake

Salt Lake City

Miles
0 5 10 15 20 25   50   75   100

0   25   50   75   100
Kilometers

Map by Atara

The possession of so much gold posed a dilemma for the Company. A horde of miners clumping through the wilderness was the last thing they wanted. Over the years they had built a monopoly in the fur trade and they knew from past experience that newcomers always disrupted this monopoly with a corresponding drop in Company profits. But the Company officers were also practical. The 800 ounces was of little commercial value in its raw state. It had first to be minted – and the nearest mint was in San Francisco. Accordingly in February 1858, the nuggets and flakes were loaded on the steamer *Otter* [which] brought the coarse gold to the mint. Word of its arrival spread like a wildfire.

Since the California gold rush had taken place only a few years previously, San Francisco was very gold conscious. This new area sounded like a good prospect. A small party of miners immediately set out for the region. They arrived on the Fraser in early spring and headed upriver past Fort Langley to Fort Hope. They asked for information but the factor, Donald Walker, in keeping with company policy, refused to talk about the country. To the free and easy going Californians, this attitude seemed strange, but it didn't discourage them.

They left Hope and camped on a bar at noon to cook lunch. While doing so, one of the party noticed particles of gold in the moss that was growing on the rocks. On the bar he washed a pan of that moss and got a prospect. After lunch they all prospected and found good pay dirt. And thus by accident was made the first discovery of what became known as the Cariboo gold rush. Hill's bar proved the richest ever discovered and was ultimately to yield $2 million. The miners promptly sent word of their find to San Francisco and the H.B.C. [Hudson's Bay Company] had triggered what it wanted least – a stampede to the river.

The first major influx was on April 25, 1858, when the paddlewheel steamer *Commodore* docked at Fort Victoria with 450 men, 60 of whom were British and the remainder Americans, Germans, Italians, and a variety of other nationalities. At that time the white population of southern Vancouver Island was about 400, for the most part employees of the H.B.C. and English colonists attempting to develop farms. The *Commodore* arrived just as Sunday church services were completed.

As citizens watched the wooden vessel, they little realized that the fur-trade era was being replaced, starting a rousing decade that would change the land and the people forever.

A reliable estimate is that in May, June and July, 23,000 people left San Francisco by sea and another 8,000 made their way overland.

Virtually overnight hundreds of tents spread from harbor side to crowd up and over the surrounding hills. Stores and saloons and other buildings appeared. Land that couldn't find a buyer for $5 an acre soared up to 100 times this price and soon to $3000 an acre.

In May 1858 Governor Douglas reported: "Many accidents have happened in the dangerous rapids of the Fraser River; a great number of canoes having been dashed to pieces and their cargo swept away by the impetuous stream, while the ill-fated adventurers who accompanied them, many have been swept into eternity."

To add to the problems of the miners there occurred a new danger – the Indians on the warpath. The tribes along the canyon resented the intrusion of the white man and wanted to keep the gold for themselves. They also claimed that the miners molested their women and were far too haughty in their attitude.

However, the Indian killings, the high water, the high cost of food, the lack of transportation, and similar hardships discouraged many men. Of the 30,000 who stampeded to the river, 25,000 returned home, referring to the Fraser in the derisive term "A Great Humbug."

But those who remained were the hardy core, men not easily discouraged, men who filtered up the rocky trench of the Fraser. Aaron Post ventured nearly 400 miles to the mouth of the Chilcotin, the first miner to prospect the area. He found gold on all bars, although lack of supplies forced him back. But he had shown the way.

Into this feverish movement came Frank Laumeister, one of the "hardy core" in a wild and untamed country. A photo of him taken in 1859 would indicate he had returned to San Francisco to pick up his family and then went back to Victoria.

During the gold rush of 1861 to 1863, the freight rates from Lillooet to the forks of the Quesnel (about 200 miles), which was the miners' base of supply at the time, were very high, 50¢ per pound and up. In fact, the charge was just what the freighters wanted to ask. Although there were several hundred head of pack mules and cayuses, they could not keep up with the demand from the mines. There were several thousand miners who had to have food at any cost, and the round trip took a full twenty days.

Art Downs had this to say:

It has been reported that when Frank Laumeister saw his Dromedary Express at the end of its journey to Richfield, he expected to clear at least $60,000 for the season. However, the difference between theory and practice soon became apparent. While the camels had their good points, they had bad points to match, and one of these was their habit of attacking anything they did not like. And it soon became apparent that they did not like anything that moved, biting and kicking anything and everything from mules to oxen, and from horses to men. Almost as bad as their bite was their smell, in fact it was so potent that it alone caused pack animals to bolt. Even washing the camels in scented water didn't help. The Dromedary Express as it became known, soon was hated throughout the Cariboo.

Another shortcoming proved to be their hoofs. They were built for sand and were no match for the rocks and hard-pan of the Fraser and Cariboo. Laumeister tried fitting them with shoes made of canvas and rawhide but this was only a part of his worries.

The miners and packers brought an avalanche of lawsuits against him for damages, and worse still, sent a petition to Governor Douglas requesting the camels be chased out of the country, but to no avail as he felt the camel caravan had as much right to participate in the transportation of supplies as other outfits.

In addition, the winters in the Cariboo were far too severe for the camels to be kept there the year round. They were

wintered lower down on the Douglas Trail.[4] Even there, they
adapted themselves marvelously to the climate, growing a
thick coat of fur to protect themselves. The fodder for winter was supplied by the owners. The rest of the year the
camels could and did forage for themselves, living much as
the deer do.[5]

One must read between the lines of Art Downs'
accusations against the camels. It has been repeated
again and again by Lee, Beale, McLeneghan, Bandmann, Vischer, and others, that the camel is a docile
and patient animal. It is also well known that with the
mules and horses which accompanied the military ex-
peditions in Texas and on Beale's trail, there were
never had disruptions or fighting among the camels
and the mules. So why should there be so much talk
about the trouble on the Cariboo Trail with the camels?

For one thing, the owners of the mules and horses
could not compete against the highly efficient, well-
organized Laumeister caravan. And the mules and
horses were never tied to each other and could run
away on the least disturbance by a rabbit or a rattle-
snake. The camels were ordinarily roped by a nose
ring to the forward animal and kept well in line by
their drivers.

The odor from the Bactrians may have been dis-
agreeable but the ill-kept mules and horses of those
times were not "sweet petunias" either. It may be that
mules and horses were frightened by the huge, ungainly, swinging, aspects of the camels, but here again,
where were their drivers in keeping them in line?

As for the damages, it may well be that packers did
not properly secure the freight to the backs of the
mules and horses, and this was always a problem

---

[4] Now known as the Harrison Trail.
[5] Downs, "Wagon Road North."

among the careless and inexperienced packers, even in military trains. Mule packers were generally thought to be of the hardened, "lickered," hot tempered, and carousing element, out to make a living on doing nothing. If freight was thrown off by the stampeding animal it was primarily caused by poorly secured merchandise. The army of the Southwest complained about this long before the Cariboo incidents. And it was usually the stubborn mules who did most of the kicking and biting, even under ordinary circumstances. It may be possible, then, that most of the lawsuits against Laumeister were fraudulent and the courts knew this, purposely delaying the cases.

Naturally the trails to the gold fields were to come under scrutiny, and plans for improvement came early. From the end of steamboat navigation at Fort Yale on the Fraser, the new strikes were 400 miles north. The route was mountainous, interspersed with valleys and gulches, and was covered for many miles with almost impenetrable underbrush. It was overlooked by mountain passes which in April harbored snow five feet deep.

Many trails were opened up by various men but they were all unsatisfactory. On the Canyon bypass, freight had to be transferred from steamer to wagon and from wagon to steamer at least eight times, and each transfer resulted in an increase in freight rates. It was evident that this route would never serve as the main thoroughfare to the Cariboo.

Fortunately there were men of vision at the head of the government, and in 1861 Governor Douglas outlined a plan as bold and imaginative as anything previously undertaken in North America. It called for construction of an eighteen-foot wagon road north for

400 miles through the rock barrier of Fraser Canyon
and across the lonely wilderness miles to the gold fields.
Considering that the permanent population of the
colony was under 7,000, the project was a tremendous
undertaking.

As a start in October of 1861, the Royal Engineers
were ordered to survey a route from Yale through the
canyon to Cook's Ferry. The same month a contract
was let for construction of the section between Boston
Bar and Lytton. In May, 1862, the Royal Engineers
started this section. Other parts of the canyon were
let to private contractors.

Art Downs notes that "in 1862, G. B. Wright and
J. C. Callbreath were awarded a contract to construct
130 miles of road from Clinton to Soda Creek, and
early in that year had progressed about twenty miles
north of Clinton. To them it appeared a logical place
for a stop-over so they built a wayside house, which
they named 70 Mile House since it was seventy miles
from the start of the Wagon Road at Lillooet. Many
of them became famous, including the 83 Mile, 100
Mile and 150 Mile." [6]

This would have been an awesome financial undertaking for people of few resources. It is very possible
that during Callbreath's negotiations for Esche's Bactrians in San Francisco, he also arranged for a substantial bank loan to be used as a guarantee to fulfill
his contract for the construction of so large a portion
of the Cariboo Wagon Road. During this period, John
Callbreath lived in Lillooet, where Laumeister started
his camel-packing venture.

Work on all sections progressed steadily and by September of 1863 the road was completed from Yale
northward 300 miles to Soda Creek, and was an instant

---

[6] *Ibid.*

success. In July, 1863, before the route was fully completed, one traveler reported that in the eighty-mile section between Yale and Cook's Ferry, he met loaded wagons, each carrying two tons of freight. In addition, there were 250 pack animals loaded with 400 pounds each.

A sternwheel steamer connected Soda Creek to Quesnel, and from Quesnel to the gold fields, travel was by trail. In 1864, construction began on a wagon road which led halfway to the gold fields, from Quesnel to Cottonwood. The next year the road was completed to Richfield, Barkerville, and Camerontown.

The improved route greatly reduced prices at the gold fields. In 1862 on William Creek flour was two dollars a pound, butter five dollars, nails five dollars, and potatoes $1.15 a pound. In 1863 and 1864, even before the road was completed, flour had dropped to 35¢ a pound, butter to $1.25, potatoes to 20-25¢, coffee to one dollar, and beef was at 40¢ a pound.[7]

The road, in its 373-mile journey from Yale to Barkerville, wound around river gorge and through rocky valley, crossed sage desert and rose to mountain top, overhung turbulent river canyons in some sections, then in others wandered by lakes with the only sound the splashing of trout feeding on evening insects.

With the completion of the Wagon Road, the mule trains began to pass away, but individual outfits survived for many years. Even in 1866 there were still over 2,000 mules being used by seventy individual outfits.

As for the camels, James B. Leighton in the Vancouver *Province* on August 1, 1926, reported, "I saw them while on my way to Barkerville in June, 1865." This would indicate that Laumeister had shifted his

[7] *Ibid.*

base of operations from Lillooet to Quesnel at the time when the Wagon Road was nearing its completion to Barkerville and Richfield, a distance of over fifty miles.

It will be of interest to sketch the lives of some of the men involved in "Laumeister's Folly," as compiled by W. E. Ireland of the Provincial Archives, Victoria, British Columbia. The ranch of Adam Heffley, for whom Heffley Creek was named, was some twelve miles above Kamloops. Here the herd of young camels was free to roam. About 1865, Heffley built his home in this area. When he died, an obituary appeared in the *Colonist* of June 11, 1872, mentioning that Heffley was a native of the United States who came to British Columbia in 1858. He was referred to as a "well-to-do" farmer on the Thompson River, having a daughter at school in Victoria and several children on the farm. An account of the funeral, performed by Dean Cridge at Christ Church Cathedral, appears in the *Colonist* of the next day. Finally, an article of September 17, 1872, relates the sale of the Heffley estate by J. Saul, administrator, to a Mr. Edwards of Lightning Creek, for $4,050; sale of stock and other property realized another $8,000 more.

Henry Ingram preempted a ranch site in January, 1864, at Grand Prairie, forty miles southeast of Kamloops (about half way to the Okanagan). He took six of the camels with him, turned them out, and they roamed with his stock, apparently without incident. He proceeded to build a large house of hewn logs, faced on the outside with dressed timber. Ingram used one of the camels named Tom to haul the logs for his house. He laid out a race track and was quite a horse fancier, breeding "Henry Welsh and Humming Bird" stock. He also kept pet bears to provide amusement. Ingram evidently was a prosperous farmer.

An article in the *Colonist* of July 17, 1873, mentions that Ingram was the first in the Thompson Valley district to celebrate the new country's Dominion Day. There is an account of the festivities, including horse racing, and an amusing tale of the escape of Ingram's pet bears. A notice of April 10, 1879 reports Ingram's death at Grand Prairie, and a further notice of April 13 names Alexander Pringle as executor for Ingram's estate.

There are a number of articles on John Cohen Callbreath in the contemporary papers. Articles in the *Colonist* of February 14 and March 15, 1862, report his residence at Cayoosh, and the purchase of twenty-three camels. Callbreath's name does not reappear until August 2, 1897, when apparently he had moved north, still a packer, probably attracted by the Klondike mines. The report says that in addition to packing, Callbreath had been engaged in a little farming to raise hay for the pack animals. The article closes by mentioning Callbreath's departure once again for the north, from Victoria.

We know more about Laumeister's life from the Provincial Archivist biography. As previously noted, Laumeister is listed as being in partnership with Charles Gowan in the 1863 *Directory*. In 1865 he was in business in the Cariboo. An advertisement placed in the June 6, 1865 *Cariboo Sentinel* read: "Laumeister and Co., merchants and dealers in provisions, liquors, and every other description of goods." And Laumeister was involved, as a trustee, in the purchase of a ranch at Cottonwood, against which he held a mortgage in August, 1865.

Laumeister appears to have been active in community affairs in the Cariboo. In September, 1865, he arranged a public dinner for A. N. Birch when the

British Columbia Colonial Secretary visited Barkerville; he played a leading role in drawing up and
presenting a petition asking for the removal of Judge
Matthew Begbie from the bench.[8] In October, 1866,
Laumeister helped raise funds for the Sisters of Char-
ity, and in July, 1867, he collected subscriptions for
the widow and orphans of a George Rowbottom.

By September, 1866, Laumeister's partnership with
A. Hoffmeister and George Steity had been dissolved
and he returned to New Westminster from the Cariboo
in November of the same year. The *Colonist* of June
23, 1868, reported that Laumeister was leaving Victoria
on the *Wright,* presumably to take up residence in the
United States. Later, his obituary said that he did
return to the United States in 1868.

Why did Laumeister want to remove Judge Begbie
from the bench? It could have been because the judge
ruled the camels off the road, but Oliver Blume dis-
counts that story: "I have found no evidence to sub-
stantiate the statement that Begbie ruled the camels
off the road. There are no contemporary newspaper
references, according to the Newspaper Index, to any
litigation caused by such accidents."[9] There were references in Judge Begbie's bench books to cases involv-
ing Laumeister, but they were concerned with the
recovery of debts, not with accidents caused by the
camels. The reputation of Judge Matthew Baille Begbie is one of an imposing, hard-working, and strict man

---

[8] M. B. Begbie, Chief Justice of British Columbia, was high-handed and
greatly disliked by the miners. Most of the officials of the Crown felt he
was a just but harsh judge. Perhaps it was a requirement in those frontier
times. He frequently overthrew lower court decisions. Begbie was knighted
by the Crown. His service to British Columbia, due to the influx of the
lawless element that was attracted by the Gold Rush was no doubt valuable.
There is no evidence that he was removed from office. There was an attempt
to remove him from office by the miners, but it failed.

[9] Oliver Blume, *Province,* Nov. 23, 1895.

who was at least partly responsible for the relatively peaceful nature of the Cariboo gold rush as compared to the one in California. The mystery of why Laumeister wanted him removed from the bench remains unsolved.

Mr. Charles Gowan, one of Laumeister's partners, made a journey to the Cariboo in 1866, to examine some of his mining claims. Gowan and some of his companions were overtaken by night, and sought shelter in a cabin beside the trail. They were heartily welcomed and soon the cheerful sound of sizzling meat was heard in the cabin. After they had eaten, their host asked them how the meat was. "Delicious," said one man. "Do you know what it was?" asked the host.

"No," came the reply.

"Camel," said the host.

"Camel!" said Mr. Gowan.

"Camel," replied the host. "There were several wandering around here for years, and we were out of meat, so we killed one. Didn't waste much, either. Tanned the hide, made a pair of saddle bags out of the humps, and the women used the hair to stuff pillows."

"Camel," said Gowan thoughtfully. "Well, once when I was shipwrecked off New Zealand, we lived for ten days on fresh air and rainwater, and I guess a camel would have looked pretty good to us then." Remembering an old insult, Gowan added, "I only hope this is the one that spat in my eye the morning he arrived in Victoria." [10]

Did the camels in general, and Laumeister's venture in particular, come to a better fate? It would appear

---

[10] Agnes E. Tate, *Daily Colonist*, Oct. 6, 1957.

so. W. W. Bride, writing in the Vancouver *Province*
of January 1, 1934, says, "The Cariboo venture did not
at all discourage would-be camel-owners. Some of the
original twenty-one were taken back to the coast and
shipped to the United States. Others were turned out
on the North Thompson River and allowed to wander
free and unmolested." Certainly Laumeister's caravan
must have had a herd of young camels ranging in age
from six months to three years old. Although there is
no record of young traveling along with their mothers,
it could have happened. The female required only a
few days to recuperate before resuming her load-
carrying duties.

As for Laumeister and Company, it appears the
venture did very well. That may be a presumption,
but we do know that Heffley and Ingram were prosperous and owned sizable farms, which certainly required large cash investments. That knowledge, com-
bined with the following analysis, suggests strongly
that the camel enterprise was a profitable undertaking.

It is not known how many males and females made
up the herd of twenty-one camels. The age of the Bactrians probably varied from between ten to twenty
years, adults at the peak of their health and strength.
On the basis of sex distribution among the wild Bactrians, two males are mated to five females. Laumeister's herd may have been composed of six males and
fifteen females, with the males supposedly able to carry
1,000 pounds each and the females 600 pounds. Perhaps some of the females were already pregnant but
not so far advanced to prevent them from carrying
a full load. Thus the caravan could have carried a
total of 15,000 pounds of food and supplies.

At thirty miles per day, the caravan could make the

round trip of 400 miles from Lillooet to Quesnel in thirteen days, or about half the time of a mule train.

Because of the rapid and safe delivery guaranteed for the camel caravan, a premium rate of 60¢ per pound was granted by the shipper. Laumeister could perhaps have been assured $9,000 per round trip. There would be no paying load on the return trip. Allowing for layover and rest, and for packing the next batch of supplies at Lillooet, the caravan might make two round trips a month for a gross of $18,000.

Freight trains usually began to move about April 1st with the beginning of warm weather, even though deep snow was still on the ground. The trips lasted until about October 1st, a total of six months, until temperatures took a sharp drop and snow began to fall in the far north Cariboo country. It is assumed that the first caravans started out about July 10th, so only one round trip was made that month. That left August and September in which to make four round trips, with a gross income for the short season of 1862 of about $45,000.

Did Laumeister and his associates make a profit? A cost analysis will give an idea of the final profits the group realized. As described earlier, the supplies for the mines were unloaded by mules, horses, and boats from Victoria at Lillooet, which was the miner's base of supply when the camels appeared on the scene.

Several hundred head of pack mules and cayuses could not keep up with the supplies needed at the mines, so the camels came in at an opportune time to prove their worth. There was a desperate need to provide for the miners at Quesnel, so the shipping price per pound of freight ranged from 50¢ to one dollar for the trip of 200 miles. It took twenty days for a round trip by mules, with no return cargo of gold at that time. This worked out at ten miles per day for the mule packers.

Prices on the Fraser at William Creek in 1862 were extremely high compared to those at Victoria, 200 miles away. Flour sold for $2 a pound, butter $5, pork and bacon $1.75, beans $1.45, potatoes $1.15, beef one dollar, sugar $1.50, nails five dollars, and tobacco six dollars a pound. That may seem high for a miner clearing eight dollars to ten dollars a day, which were considered good earnings. But the price of food alone amounted on the average to half of his wages, in addition to other expenses. Everything was paid for in gold dust or nuggets. As a rule, flour, sugar, and potatoes were shipped by the hundredweight in barrels or sacks.

As for the expenses, Laumeister had paid $6,000 for twenty-three camels, losing two on the way. The cost of sending them by steamer from San Francisco to Victoria, and by steamers and barges to Port Douglas must have come to $1,000, including feed.

The wages of packers and a cook varied from $11 to $125 a month, in addition to board. The trainmaster frequently received $150 per month. Laumeister and his associates must have assumed some of these duties, with the help of the two drivers, Assan and Ali, at $25 a month. In addition, there were six laborers at two dollars per day. Two men would oversee each of the three caravans, which were roped by nose rings.

There was also the cost of providing thick leather bootees for the camels' sensitive feet, possible at $1 each. The stony Cariboo roads were not adaptable for the soft-padded feet, and the Bactrians would soon become lame without protection. To keep the feet of twenty-one camels in good condition, there must have been a constant demand for the heavy canvas and leather shoes of perhaps 1,000 units per six-month period.

Since Lillooet was the start of the trail and the headquarters for Laumeister's company, he must have purchased land for a caravansary enclosure to provide pasturage for the camels. It is assumed he purchased at least five acres of rich pasture for at least $500 per acre. With a fence around it to keep the camels confined and the wolves outside, and an office from which to carry on the freight business, the total expenses must have been about $3,500. The caravansary could then provide a resting place for the camels in the summer between trips, and protection from the weather in the winter. The cost of feed and water was practically nil.

The cost of the camels, their maintenance, shipping, and the price of land and structures may be summarized as follows:

1 master	. $1,800 per year
2 packers	3,000
1 cook	1,200
2 caretakers	300
Shoes	1,000
Land, etc.	3,500
Camels, Shipping . . .	7,000

This would yield a total cost of about $18,000 for 1862, and a net profit of about $27,000, with all obligations paid off.

With such profit, Laumeister and his associates lowered the cost of packing to 40¢ per pound for the 1863 season. They may also have been reacting to the great agitation against their monopoly. For a full six months the income would be about $6,500 for each

round trip, or about $78,000 for the season, less $7,500
maintenance, leaving a net income of around $71,000.
By the second year, Laumeister and his company could
have achieved their dream of making $60,000 per year.
At the end of 1865, they could have made a total of
about $240,000. Assuming the settlement of some law-
suits came to about $40,000, the partners would still
clear $200,000, a considerable fortune in those days.

This seems to confirm statements that Ingram and
Heffley were prosperous farmers and Laumeister something of a capitalist.

A look at the competition is instructive. A good,
healthy mule capable of carrying 250 to 400 pounds
would cost from $250 to $400. The aparejo, a leather
sack filled with straw tied to the mule's back, was used
in place of the pack saddle. Freight was lashed to it
with a diamond hitch. A white mare usually led the
train, but the mules were not tied together in any way;
each knew its place and kept it throughout the trip.

The crew usually consisted of a cook and a cargadore
who had overall command, plus one man or driver for
every eight to ten animals. The train traveled about
fifteen miles a day, but since stops had to be made
where there was food and water, some days saw more
ground covered than others. A round trip from Yale
to the goldfields took about two months, so there were
about three trips per season.

We have noted that twenty-one camels carried over
155,000 pounds of freight. At an average of 325
pounds per mule, a pack train of about 46 mules would
be required to transport the same load. Assuming the
freight rate was 60¢ a pound, the owners of the mule
train would take in $9,000 on a round trip. At an
average of fifteen miles per day, it would take them

about a month to make the round trip from Lillooet to Quesnel and back, yielding a gross income of $54,000 for six round trips in 1862.

But the expense was something else. The cost of twenty-three males at $400 would be $9,200; for twenty-three females at $250, the cost would be $5,750, making a total outlay of around $15,000.

Other expenses would be as follows:

    1 cargadore . . . . . $1,800 per year
    6 packers 9,000
    1 cook 1,200

That amounts to $12,000 per year. The cost of feed at the time was betwen 6¢ and 7¢ a pound, or an average of 6.5¢ for barley or oats. At ten pounds per mule per day, the daily cost would be about $30 for the forty-six mules, or around $11,000 per year. Leasing land at Lillooet to pasture the animals would have cost about $300, or $3,600 for a year. The total cost then would then be $41,600, meaning the entire operation would net about $12,000.

For 1863, with the cost of the mules written off, the packers would net about $27,000, provided they were paid 60¢ a pound for the load. Obviously feed was the most expensive item, a cost Laumeister did not have to consider. If the mule train owners continued to get 60¢ a pound, they made about $95,000 for the four years.

No wonder the opposition resented Laumeister's operation. Not only did Laumeister make more money, but the packers suffered more losses by not tying the animals. It is understandable that they wanted to freeze him out.

When the Wagon Road was completed in 1865, long ox teams began to appear. They were pulling wagons which carried a ton of freight per ox; their pace was very slow, averaging about six to twelve miles a day. These wagons sealed the fate of the mules and the camels in the Cariboo country.

As mentioned, Laumeister and his associates could have made a fortune if the freighting business had continued on a high level as late as 1865. Now let us assume a more conservative and different approach to the economic operation of the Bactrians.

It was noted that five businessmen formed a partnership with Laumeister to import camels into the Cariboo in the early part of 1861, after perhaps hearing the report of Ingram and Heffley, who had spent weeks in Nevada with Bandmann's camels. The partners were told how much it would cost to purchase them and bring them to Victoria by ship.

There is no hint as to how John Callbreath, a packer, came to be selected as the agent to procure the animals, but he undoubtedly was given full authority to draw a draft on a bank in Victoria to pay Bandmann the $6,000 fee to obtain the twenty-three Bactrians. Callbreath must have received at least five percent commission, or about $300, for his part of the transaction. And someone must have paid Heffley and Ingram about $500 for their survey of the camels while traveling with Bandmann in Nevada, and for their consultation and selection of the best specimens with Callbreath. Transporting the camels to Victoria and beyond probaly cost at least $1,000.

We may assume that when the total expenses of bringing the Bactrians to Lillooet came to $7,800, the five partners contributed at least $5,000 and Laumeister another $5,000.

In the meantime, perhaps without serious notice by the partners, the construction of a wagon road started in March 1862, and by September of 1863, the 300-mile stretch between Yale and Soda Creek was completed. It must have been sometime between 1863 and 1864 that the partners realized the significance of the new road's impact on their freighting business. By the end of 1864, the cost of food at the gold fields had been reduced to one-fourth of the prices in 1862, caused entirely by the introduction of the huge freight wagons drawn by oxen.

As indicated earlier, the partners could have had a net profit of $27,000 at the end of 1862, and of $71,000 in 1863. Perhaps with reduced freight charges in 1864, they may have netted $15,000, for a total of $110,000. Out of this some $30,000 worth of lawsuits may have been paid because of stampedes set off by the ill-smelling Bactrians.

It may be that sometime in 1862, Heffley and Ingram also became partners with Laumeister, making at least seven partners. Of the $80,000 remaining after the lawsuits, the partners may have received half of that amount, or about $6,000 each, with Laumeister getting the remaining $40,000 when the partnership was dissolved. And it is very likely that Laumeister took possession of all the camels.

Laumeister's biography indicates he was conducting a large business in June, 1865 in the Cariboo. He may have been using the camels to carry freight from Quesnel to Barkerville, a distance of 50 miles. Laumeister was active in many business and social activities, which indicated that he was financially well-off.

Even if the company did not make $200,000, this conservative appraisal indicates that the partners made a substantial profit, and the head of the company did very well on "Laumeister's Folly."

This was not the end of the camels. In 1864, news

of another gold strike came out to civilization and Wild Horse Creek was on everyone's lips. The long and difficult packing into the little town of Fisherville at the mouth of the creek again led men to speculate on methods of improved transportation. The solution was camels. Again the double-humped pack animals swung up and down the trails of British Columbia. They were chiefly used on the Kootenay road via the Dewdney trail,[11] through Princeton. Nor was the northwestern United States to escape another visit from the caravans of the impertinent, gentle Bactrians.

[11] Constructed by engineer E. Dewdney in 1865.

3

Bactrians in Washington Idaho and Montana

Our records of the use of camels in the northwest portion of the United States is sketchy, but we do know that they were used frequently. Their services were proposed as early as 1819.

Fred Wilbur Powell, writing in the *Oregon Historical Quarterly* in March of 1917, said that

> While [Senator Thomas Hart] Benton [1] was writing of the necessity of a transcontinental route to the Columbia River country, another man was developing the same idea. This man (perhaps the editor, John S. Skinner) in an anonymous article, which appeared in the July 9, 1819, number of the *American Farmer* of Baltimore, proposed "the Bactrian camel as a beast of burthen for cultivators, and for transportation across the continent, to the Pacific Ocean." Under this head he presented a glowing picture of the possibilities of the Northwest, its fertile soil, its great quantities of excellent timber, its productive fisheries, and its salubrious climate as indicated by its numerous and robust population of Indians . . .
>
> He therefore proposed the establishment of communications by the most direct route and the use of the Bactrian camel, whose good qualities he proceeded to set forth at great length, and concluded with the question, "Why not add the majestic, long lived, placid, and valuable Bactrian camel to the number of the auxiliary laborers and carriers for the active citizens of the nation?"

[1] Thomas Hart Benton was a Senator from the state of Missouri, a booster of the first order for Manifest Destiny, and the father-in-law of John C. Fremont, the western explorer.

When we come to inquire as to the source from which the unknown sponsor of the Bactrian camel obtained his information as to the Northwest, the name of Benton suggests itself.

Though we do not know if that suggestion was ever followed, we do know that placer gold discoveries were made in Oro Fino (now Orofino) and at Pierce City in northern Idaho in October 1861, and that the camels would follow later. The finds then spread to Hell Gate near Missoula, Montana, and by 1865, to Virginia City, Montana, and Last Chance Gulch, near Helena.

These were the years when Laumeister and his associates thrived in the Cariboo country, where the well-known mining communities were fairly close together. But when two-thirds of the Bactrian herd was sold early in 1865 to be used in the new gold fields in Washington Territory, the mule packers and freight wagons were already crowded on the long trails. The price of carrying goods from Umatilla, Oregon, on the Columbia River, to the Boise Basin in Idaho, a distance of 300 miles, ranged from 40¢ to 80¢ a pound.

The competition from long-established packers posed a problem to the late comers, among whom were the owners of the camel caravans.

The chronological order of the movements of the camel caravans comes to us entirely from the memory of those few who got to know the entire mining region. Mines were spread far apart over difficult, high mountain trails. There were no roads, except for the far-from-practical Mullan's Road,[2] which stretched from

---

[2] Named for Lt. John Mullan, U.S. Army. Mullan had an active part in the government railroad survey of 1853. He constructed the road from Fort Benton to Walla Walla using a government appropriation of $30,000. The road was built from 1859 to 1862. It was cut through prairies, dense forests, and over steep mountains, with bridges and containments. The completed highway was 25 to 30 feet wide, and cost $230,000.

Walla Walla, Washington, on the Snake River, to Helena and Fort Benton (Montana) on the Missouri River, a distance of 700 miles.

Perhaps the earliest item noting camels in the Northwest was published in the Walla Walla *Statesman* on March 12, 1864:

> A PACK CAMEL. In the train that left here this week for the Kootenai mines is something new, in the shape of a pack animal, for this country – an Arabian Camel. Mr. Wm. Henry, of the Bitter Root Ferry is the fortunate owner of the animal; he obtained it from parties recently from the Caribou region. A number of these animals were shipped to that country about a year ago to be used as pack animals, but owing to the stony formation of the country they became foot sore, and their owners had to decide the investment a non-paying one. Mr. H. had 400 pounds on his camel and thinks he can make profitable use of him in packing between here and Kootenai, as the country to be traveled over is most of the way but little unlike that of his native desert.

Then in the *Montana Post* (Virginia City, Montana) on June 3, 1865, a prophecy came true.

> DROMEDARIES [3]
>
> We phophecied a dromedary extension to Montana, and here they are – six of them. They will, say the posters, carry ten children each, pack 1000 pounds, kneel, and arise at the word of command and so forth and so forth. The exhibition will take place at the Gibson House, Idaho Street, on Saturday, from 2 P.M. till 6 P.M. and on Sunday from 10 A.M. till 6 P.M. Everybody and friends are going. What a splendid transport train they would make. The aborigine would be scared to death and each warrior would feel for a hump on his back.

The same paper reported a local hunter's mistake on July 1, 1865:

---

[3] These had to be Bactrians. The reporter was in error by calling them Dromedaries, as only Bactrians could carry 1000 lb. loads.

Shot the Wrong Bird

One of the dromedaries which lately came into the territory, was quietly grazing near Snowshoe Creek, when a hunter of game observed the wonderful brute. Thinking he was about to contribute a new name to the list of American Quadrupeds, he fired. Down sank "the ship of the desert" and up ran the hunter. On discovering the anatomical peculiarities, Nimrod evaporated with rapidity. Being overtaken by the owner, and informed in a very pointed and energetic manner that he had shot one of his pursuer's camels, with inimitable nonchalance he exclaimed "Well, mister, you can have the camel if it's yours." On mature reflection the camel shooter has determined to go for elephants on his next hunt.

Once again from the *Montana Post* on July 29, 1865, we hear of wonder in Helena.

On Saturday last quite an excitement was created in town by the appearance of a train of dromedaries opposite Stoke and Lewis store. In the presence of a large crowd of idlers and spectators attracted by the novel spectacle, "the ships of the desert, which exhibited the most lamb-like docility, were made to kneel down, for the purpose of receiving their burden of 600 pounds of flour each. As soon as the load was packed securely, they arose and travelled off with as much ease as a cayuse pony would if ladened with a miner's outfit. Their destination was Washington Gulch which is accessible, as far as freight is concerned by pack animals only.

One observer who saw the herd in front of the store of Gaston and Simpson in Helena in 1866 recalled they used to carry enormous loads. "They would be loaded with sacks of flour until you couldn't see anything of the animals except their heads. They would carry all you could pile on them, and never show that the pack was any load for them at all. They would be loaded at the gulches with gold dust in nail kegs and bring the dust to Helena. They would go up and over the mountains in the roughest and steepest places and never refuse to keep moving along in their slow, deliberate way." [4]

One cargo the camels were to carry was more necessary than gold. The miners had to have food.

James Polk Miller, who was a packer before the camels came, noted in his diary that May and June of 1865 were severe, with cold, snow, and hail. And well he knew. He had brought 660 dozen eggs to Virginia City from Salt Lake City on June 10, 1865. His fragile goods sold for 90¢ a dozen, then dropped to 60¢, but by December 2, 1865, they had risen again to $2.50 a dozen. Much of southern Montana's food supply came via this route. Eggs, butter, and flour were exceedingly scarce.

The *Montana Post* of May 8, 1865, reports the bread riot in southern Montana. "Flour had gone up to $40 [per 100 lbs]. At Nevada City, on a Sunday the previous week, the mob bought flour all day at $25.00 dust. In Virginia City, the mob raged through Sunday and Monday, stump speakers haranguing it, both to inflame and to moderate. Finally, such a show of resistance to the demand of the people was organized that the idea [of a riot] was quietly given up. Destitution does not seem to have reached the pitch where men were willing to purchase bread with blood. And so it ended."

Those were the circumstances into which the camels were called to carry food supplies into inaccessible towns where gold was king and yet the people had little to eat.

Even before the camels appeared, pack trains were not the only means used to move freight. Freight, as well as the miners themselves, could be carried by

---

[4] Joel E. Ferris, *Spokesman Review.* (Aug. 1, 1954).

wagon and even by boat as far as the advanced trans-shipment points, from where they went on by mule. Freight rates were high and returns to the packers very satisfactory. Some indication of just how satisfactory they were is clear in a message to Congress forwarded by the Washington Territorial Legislature in 1866. It stated, among other things, that "no less than six thousand mules have left Walla Walla and the Columbia River loaded with freight for Montana." Moreover, the *Montana Post* estimated that during the spring and summer of the same year there were between 8,000 and 10,000 pack animals operating in the Montana freight trade.

Freight rates by 1866 from Walla Walla to Virginia City were 30¢ to 40¢ a pound. The first new flour to arrive in Virginia City went for $58 to $62 a hundred-weight sack. It took as many men to freight goods to the miners as it took miners to work the mines. They transported $12 million in goods that year.

We can reconstruct the movements of Laumeister's Bactrians from various sources, beginning with the recollections of James Watt. In July and October 1928, two articles appeared in the *Washington Historical Quarterly,* both by William Lewis and James Watt. In the introduction, the editor stated:

> William S. Lewis, Historian of the Spokane County Pioneers' Association, through interviews and conferences with James W. Watt during the past two years, has secured this illuminating and helpful narrative of forceful and dramatic experiences during the placer mining days in Washington Territory, including those great areas later organized into Idaho and Montana. Mr. Watt was a very young "Forty-niner." He was born in Salem, Ohio, on May 31, 1843, and with his parents crossed the plains to California in the big year of the gold rush. After the vigorous experiences here related,

Mr. Watt settled at his present home in the Lance Hills district, near Cheney, Spokane County, Washington. Mr. Lewis has welded together the various interviews and recorded the entire narrative in the language of Mr. Watt. Mr. Lewis says that Mr. Watt is the first pioneer he has encountered who actually saw the pack train of camels in the Northwest.

Watt went to the Washington Territory for the first time in 1860. He was at The Dalles, Oregon, when news of the discovery of the Pierce City gold mines was heard. Many of the men in his neighborhood had been in the California mines. At Walla Walla he joined the pack train of the D. M. Jesse Company and went into the mines with it, via Lewiston, Idaho, reaching the mining town, Oro Fino, about July 20, 1861. From that time on, Watt was a packer until about 1867. During that period he saw numerous camel caravans and heard stories about them, all of which are recorded in the articles.

As mentioned before, there was another gold strike on Wild Horse Creek in 1864. The packers operated from Fort Hope to the Kootenay road and on to Fort Steele. Watt said he saw a pack train of five or six camels on the Moyie River in 1866. It was owned by a French Canadian. He kept one camel in the Wild Horse Creek area and for two or three years it lived on the range. This could mean the original caravan was composed of six camels; then when the French Canadian sold it he kept one for himself. The remaining five went to Walla Walla about 1867, probably following the old Indian Trail (now Highway 395).

Sometime in 1865 or 1866, a caravan of six camels was used in freighting from Helena to Walla Walla by way of Missoula and the Coeur d'Alene mountains. This route brought the camels over the Mullan Road

to the Columbia River boat landings and to Walla
Walla. It was there that a firm of freighters owned
several different camel caravans, as stated by James
Watt. It could have been about 1867 that he saw two
camel pack trains, one of about six animals and the
other of about twelve, making a trip over the Oregon
emigrant trail to Bannock City (now Idaho City),
Idaho. The roads were lined with pack trains, saddle
horses, stagecoaches, and people afoot or on horseback
leading pack animals, all going to or from the mines.
Part of the road went over alkali flats and the dust
stirred up by one party did not get a chance to settle
before the next party came along. Onto this crowded
Oregon Trail came several camel caravans. Enroute
they stampeded a large freight outfit and caused so
much damage they were withdrawn from the trail
at Bannock City and, according to Watt, sent out toward Salt Lake City. However, in another article published in the April 15, 1928, *Spokesman Review,* Watt
says: "After being on the trail out of Walla Walla for
some time, the camel train was taken down on the
Winnemucca trail and at last accounts of it were heard
in Nevada." This appears to contradict his statement
that the camels were sent to Salt Lake City, but we
may have an answer later on.

Perhaps another reason the camels were released
was that the season was very short, and was followed
by severe winters. There was also a need to provide
shelter to care for the young and to protect the adults
from the cold weather after they shed their heavy
winter mane, which left them completely naked.

Some of the experiences of the packers on the Walla
Walla trail into Montana afforded abundant material
for fireside tales by eye witnesses to various incidents.

One man told of having an entire load of breakable merchandise wrecked by the stampede of his pack train when the horses spied the camels coming down the trail toward them. The oldtimer said that it was as easy to stop a blizzard or an avalanche as it was to head off a pack train of mules or horses frightened by a camel caravan. Another camel train stampeded a pack train loaded with a cargo of whiskey destined for the saloons near Hell Gate. The casks were all sprung or broken, the whiskey leaked away, and the residents of that area were compelled to drink water until a new shipment came.

The Bactrians carried merchandise to the gold-producing camps on Bear Gulch, Gold Creek, and Deer Lodge (Montana). They also hauled gold dust from the mines. One camel alone could carry several thousand dollar's worth. Among the famous loads carried by the Bactrians in Montana was the first shipment from the Bonanza claim at Alder Gulch (Virginia City), a strike which the original finder, Edgar, is said to have sold for $14.85 and a plug of tobacco.

After being used about Helena for some months the camel train was placed on the Walla Walla trail out of Missoula, and thereafter made regular runs to the western country instead of doing local packing among the Montana camps.

As usual, the camels were unpopular with the other packers. Horses and mules stampeded at the sight and smell of the strange animals. More than one packer resorted to the severest language in his adequate vocabulary of cuss words, when rounding up his scattered herd. The poor beasts would leave the road with utter disdain of ceremony as soon as the camels came into sight, and there were many accidents.

The Indians had, of course, never heard of such creatures, and it required constant vigilance and explanations on the part of the owner of the outfit to keep the Indians from shooting his strange imported stock.

The camels saw a lot of service on Mullan Road, which turned out to be unimportant for military use but proved invaluable to overland travelers and settlers. The latter could come by water two-thirds of the distance west, via the Missouri River from St. Louis to Fort Benton, then cross the Rockies on the Mullan Road. In the summer of 1862 a party of 300 emigrants, Oregon-bound in their covered wagons, took the road, and in 1865, 20,000 people passed over it. Mullan was promoted to captain in 1862 and honored by a vote of thanks from Washington Territory.

It is unclear exactly as to how the camels were used during the period, but part of the story can be pieced together from several observations. John Hailey's manuscript, *History of Idaho* (1910), says that the camels in burden caravans were often tied head to tail with an iron ring inserted in the nose. They travelled in files of about seven animals with the driver riding ahead on a donkey or a camel, and the last camel wearing a bell so the driver could tell by listening if the chain were broken. We shall see that this indicates the use of several pack trains in the Montana area.

According to William S. Lewis, the first caravan of seven camels came into Helena in May of 1865; it was one of those animals which was later shot by accident. In 1866 or 1867, James Watt saw a camel pack train on the Moyie River near the Canadian border. It was owned by a Frenchman, accompanied by a packer and a cook, who was then packing from Fort Hope to the Wild Horse mines with six camels.

Another man, William Henry, was using a camel for transportation to the mines. Judge F. H. Woody, an overland traveller, saw a camel train packing between Walla Walla and Fort Benton with seven camels, one of which drowned in the Missoula River at the Mullan Road crossing.

James Watt then records that he saw two camel caravans, one of six animals and one of twelve. They were making a trip from Walla Walla over the Boise Trail in 1867. They may have been the remnants of Laumeister's twenty-one camels.

It would appear then, that there were three groups of camels used on the Walla Walla, Wild Horse, Fort Benton, and Boise trails, so perhaps Laumeister's camels were broken into three caravans. They may have been managed first by Laumeister, Ingram, and Heffley, or by other people, and sent across the trails at intervals to partially avoid encounter with the mules and horses of other trains. The three groups of camels may have been sold separately to packers in the Walla Walla area beginning in 1865. The small "family" caravans of a few males and females would conform to the usual practice in Asiatic countries.

Again from William S. Lewis, we may have a good explanation of the absence of facts about the camels. Lewis says that there was "a peculiar dearth of news on the subject in local newspapers of the time. Analysis of the situation establishes that these local newspapers and readers were then principally concerned with 'outside news' from the Coast, and from the Eastern states on business, politics and the progress of the Civil War. Local news and events, which everyone knew, were therefore seldom mentioned in the local press." [5]

---

[5] William S. Lewis, *Wash. Hist. Qtly.*, Seattle, Wash., 1928.

The mystery still remains. How did the Bactrians finally reach Nevada? As mentioned before, after a stampede on the Boise trail the camels were sent south by either Salt Lake or Winnemucca.

James Watt was packing out of Umatilla, which was the center for the heavy freight business in eastern Oregon, southern Idaho, and northwest Nevada. During 1862 and 1863, Indians caused Watt considerable trouble, and during this period freight was carried inland from Umatilla to as far as Winnemucca (then called Big Bend), Nevada. It is of interest to note that the Central Pacific Railroad tracks reached this community in 1868.

The possibility exists that the Bactrian caravans did cross the Salt Lake area and then took the Overland Stage route westward through Nevada to Virginia City.

The following note is taken from the *Oregonian,* February 14, 1927, and is titled, "Camels Declared a Success," written by an oldtimer, Fred S. Perrine:

> . . . in the summer of 1865 a few camels were brought from Nevada into Montana, loaded with merchandise. One was drowned while crossing the Missoula River, a short distance below Missoula, and another was shot by a hunter who had never seen a camel and thought it was a moose. None of the camels which were taken into Montana were of the United States government herd. These were part of a lot of camels imported from Asia to San Francisco in 1860-61. These camels were used to pack salt from a marsh in Esmeralda county, Nevada, to the Washoe silver mines, and were used as late as 1876.
>
> The camels used in the Caribou and Fraser river regions were part of the same lot, although one authority states that three were of the original United States government herd.

There are several interesting items here that may

help clear up some confusion not understood before. As will be noted later on, no camels were brought in from Nevada. However, Perrine does reveal that the camels were Bactrians, which indicates that they were from Laumeister's herd. This clears up several inaccurate news items which stated that two dromedaries were seen in Portland and in Salem, Oregon. In the *Portland Oregonian* on August 5th and 6th, 1863, the owners claimed that they brought their animals down from the Cariboo via Victoria, and that the two dromedaries were later being taken to the Salmon River.[6]

As to how the camels ended up in Nevada, there is evidence that Brigham Young, the Mormon leader, was already familiar with the beasts being used as pack animals, and that it was Young who initially recommended that the camels be used to transport timber from the California Sierras to build the Union Pacific Railroad. In his *Pioneering the Union Pacific,* Edgar Ames says:

> Taking the advice of Brigham Young, late in the year of 1865, Samuel Reed made a preliminary survey from Salt Lake City, passing north of Salt Lake into the former Lake Bonneville, for 209 miles to the dead-ended Humboldt River in Nevada. Although grades did not exceed 60 feet, the general area was a saline-alkaline plain between mountain ranges, with little fresh water and none over one 60-mile stretch. Timber was very scarce, and there was no sign of coal. He recommended building the up from the California border eastward to solve the lumber problem, using camels.

On July 5, 1862, President Abraham Lincoln signed the Pacific Railway Act, in which Congress pledged a $500 million loan and millions of acres of the Great American Desert toward the Railroad's completion.

---

[6] The Salmon River empties into the Snake River which forms the border between Washington and Idaho.

The Civil War was then in its gloomiest period, as the Battle of Bull Run had endangered Washington, Maryland, and the surrounding country. In September, the Union Pacific Railroad and Telegraph Company was created at Chicago to compete with its rival, the Central Pacific Railroad Company of California. The ground-breaking ceremony for the C.P. was celebrated in Sacramento on January 8, 1863, and a similar ceremony was held for the U.P. at Omaha, Nebraska on December 2, 1863.

By the end of 1866, the U.P. had completed 305 miles of track west from Omaha and the C.P. had begun preparation to cross the Sierra Nevada summit near Cisco, 100 miles east of Sacramento.

Under the terms of the supplementary charter of 1864, a great incentive was given both railroads to put down the most mileage possible. In addition to land and bonds based on mileage, there was traffic to be won around Salt Lake City and in all of Mormon country.

The Central was pushing northeast along the Humboldt River through a dreary land inhabited only by Indians, while the redwood, pine and cedar railroad ties were flowing down the slopes of the Sierras. The desert country furnished nothing. For 500 miles there was not a tree large enough to make a board and scrub pine and juniper could not provide ties.

Leland Stanford, president of the Central Pacific, contracted with Brigham Young early in 1867 for his legion to grade 160 miles west from Ogden to meet the incoming C.P. rails crossing through Nevada.

The Union Pacific had also launched a grading contract with Young, covering 220 miles west of Ogden to Humboldt Wells (now Wells, Nevada). Superintendent Samuel Reed was in charge of this westward work. The entire route was surveyed by the U.P. as far as the California line. When the U.P. recalled all its workers back to Ogden to rush its rails to Promontory Summit late in 1868, the U.P. grade skirted the C.P. grade westward for 200 miles, and had laid rails 80 miles east of Wells. It is estimated that a million dollars was spent on that 80 miles. Very likely this was the route over which the camels were used to haul ties from the Sierras to Humboldt Wells.

Brigham Young also contracted to grade and build the U.P. road from the head of Echo Canyon toward the Salt Lake Valley for 54 miles, and to continue around the north end of Salt Lake. By the end of 1868 the Mormon workers were attacking the grade to Promontory Point, so that the rails along this grade from Ogden would hasten westward before the Central Pacific drove the spikes in its own gap. In all the construction of the U.P. roads over 4,000 Mormons were employed, with several million dollars going into Young's tabernacle.

We have found no mention of camels, however, except as noted. Young's recommendation was apparently in reference to hauling ties, which were usually eight feet long, eight inches wide, and six inches thick. In green timber, that would have been about eighty-five pounds. The Bactrians could carry at least eight ties for a total of nearly 700 pounds each. The caravans would have made an efficient shuttle service to carry the ties in Nevada.

4

The Nevada Sequel

Camels could have served the railroads well in Nevada, but as in places they had worked before, freight business to the mines turned out to be their main job. However, in the Comstock Lode area of Nevada that job had some variations.

Those odd veins and pieces of black rock which overlaid the seams and wedges of the ground were at first only a nuisance to the miners, who had eyes for gold only. However, some curious visitors had them assayed, and that started the Comstock rush. The ore had shown a value of $3000 in silver and $870 in gold per ton, and the rich silver came in chlorides and sulfides.

Gold is relatively easy to extract from its matrix, but silver is another question. It must be reduced from its ore, and this was no easy process. First the rock was crushed, mixed with water, quicksilver, and salt, then stirred, heated and separated. It was not a job for a man with a pan or a sluice box.

By 1861, two years after the first assay, eighty-six companies with capital stock of almost $62 million were in operation in the area. One of their problems was salt. Eliot Lord, in *Comstock Mining and Miners,* published in 1883, put it this way:

> The folly of transporting salt across the Sierras to a Territory whose soil differs little from that of Sodom was early seen, and provision was soon made for the supply of this staple from Nevada marshes. A train of nine Bactrian camels bore

loads across the desert from the forks of the Walker River in 1861, and in 1863 two companies were organized to quarry a salt plain at Sand Springs on the Humboldt River. Sixty tons were furnished monthly by one of these companies after beginning work, in June, 1864, at a cost to the consumer of $80 per ton instead of $120, the price asked previously for salt imported from California.

In the conduct of this business an interesting trial was made of the comparative efficiency of camels and mules as pack animals in the Nevada desert. On level, well-beaten trails the camels traveled as rapidly as mules, and over plains of deep sand as fast as oxen on a good road. Their average load was slightly under 450 pounds, which was nearly double the weight of an ordinary mule pack. The cost of their fodder was small, as they ate greedily all kinds of grass, thistles, tules, and willows, and were particularly fond of the acrid greesewood.[1]

The camels Lord referred to must have been Bactrians, since Samuel McLeneghan's Arabians had yet to appear in Nevada. Let us take a new inventory of the camels Esche brought to San Francisco. As mentioned before, there were forty-five Bactrians left after the severe passage from Siberia to San Francisco.

	added	sold	total
Arrived in San Francisco, July 1860	15		15
Died by time of first auction		2	13
Sold at auction, Oct. 1860		3	10
Sold by Bandman (consignment), Sept. 1861		9	1
Arrived in San Francisco, Nov. 1861	10		11
Arrived on *Dollart,* Jan. 1862	20		31
Bought by Callbreath, April 1862		23	8
Possible births in unsold herd by 1863	7		15
Bought by Chevalier, March 1864		15	0

Arthur Woodward noted in *Camels and Surveyors in Death Valley* that fifteen camels, purchased by Marius Chevalier, a Frenchman, crossed over the Sierra

---

[1] Eliot Lord, *Comstock Mining and Miners,* reprinted by Howell North (Berkeley, Ca., 1959).

in March of 1864. This group could have included the remaining camels. They must have joined Bandmann's group at Chevalier's ranch, if so.

The *Territorial Enterprise* of May 10, 1862, noted the arrival in Virginia City, Nevada, of two tons of salt by camel train for the Central Mill from a salt marsh 150 miles away. The camels were driven by Mexicans "who seem not to know the difference between a mule and a camel." Assuming these were Bandmann's nine camels, this would indicate that each animal carried an average of 450 pounds of salt. The marsh from which it came was the famous Columbus Salt Marsh field in Esmeralda County, Nevada. Near it the Rhodes Salt Marsh (Mineral County) was discovered in 1862, some 150 miles southeast of Virginia City. Camel trains out of Rhodes became so numerous that a Virginia City ordinance phohibited the humped beasts from entering the city during certain hours of the day in order to prevent horses and mules from stampeding. The salt continued to come. Teels Marsh was started in early 1867. The settlement of Marietta was established on its north shore, and the salt was sent by long camel trains to the mills near Virginia City, and by pack mules to Aurora.

The Comstock mills consumed great quantities of salt, though no general agreement was evident in the manner of it use or effectiveness. Some operators applied salt with scientific sophistication; others used it naively in the same manner as early millers, who lacking any knowledge in chemistry, even tried tobacco juice, decoction of sagebrush, and other equally absurd ingredients. The succeeding century has not settled the controversy of early use of salt.

The mills bought several thousand tons of salt each year and though one company invested over $100,000 to outfit seventy large teams to transport the product eighty miles for delivery, other teams had to be hired to assist – with extra freight bills running from $10,000 to $15,000 per week. At the time, the uniform price for salt delivered at the mill was $60 per ton, substantially less than its cost from previous sources at San Francisco and Rhodes, Nevada.

And it could be delivered at still less from closer sources. After discovery of the Eagle Salt Marsh [2] in 1869, salt production at such places as Sand Springs practically ceased, but that same year newly organized companies began exploiting a borax deposit on Four Mile Flat. Salt mining continued for many years.

The price of $60 per ton works out to 3¢ a pound. This must have been when the huge freighting-wagons came into use. But in the early 1860s the price was probably ten times that amount, which was well within the range of mule trains and camel caravans.

Salt was not the only new cargo camels carried in the Comstock days. Cheap fuel was a pressing need in the mining districts, and the neighboring hills were so scantily clad with trees that it was necessary to turn to the Sierras. The stunted wood of the Nevada hills drove several hundred laborers into the business of cutting and hauling wood. During the summer months cedar sold at from $13 to $15 a cord and pine from $16 to $18. The leading mining companies, taught by the costly experience of a severe winter, showed some foresight in providing a stock of fuel for winter use. But the easy-going townsfolk were generally less

---

[2] According to David F. Myrick in *Railroads of Nevada and Eastern California*, Vol. I, Eagle Salt Works was less than fifty miles from Reno and about fifteen miles east of Wadsworth, Nevada, on the old Central Pacific rail line. Discovered by B. F. Leete, operations were started two years later. Salt was recovered by sun-drying saline spring water in a number of ponds covering some ten acres.

provident. When an early frost gave warning of snows to come, the price of wood quickly went up to $20 to $30 a cord. Trains of loaded carts could be seen every day coming from the Palmyra district and El Dorado Cañon,[3] the chief sources of supply. Troops of donkeys with bundles of sticks piled high above their ears scrambled down the steep hill slopes.

In 1866, 120 Chinese were employed as wood merchants, and one firm's daily sales amounted to $300. A cord of wood doled by their measurement cost from $33 to $48, for a profit of $20. In a season of exceptional severity, as the winter of 1866-67 was, the wood went for even more. In 1866, it was reported that 200,000 cords of wood were delivered to consumers in the district. The daily use by mills crushing ore was 378 cords, for which the mills paid $10 per cord, or nearly $4,000 a day.

During the years immediately following the discovery of the lode, the towns that sprang up faced another problem. At first water was in sufficient but irregular supply from the short tunnels that honeycombed the hillsides. But the population was growing. In a short time, mining companies whose search for ore went unrewarded found an unlooked for source of revenue in the barren rock. Water was as readily saleable as ore, and the demand for it was great. In some instances, the engines at the mines raised all the water required for the boilers from their own shafts. But the water was generally impure, and this led to a rapid formation of scale.

Thus, while the mines had plenty of water, the miners were always in danger of thirst. The supply usually lasted, barely, until the spring runoffs. As Virginia City grew, the peril of drought increased

---

[3] Both of these places are located a few miles south of the Comstock.

with each succeeding year. Yearly, the same events repeated – flumes and pipes ran full in the spring and were half empty in autumn.

When there was a water shortage, the mules and horses had to have their rations strictly regulated. But this was not a problem with the camels, for they could go for days without water, and without complaint. It was a strong factor in their favor when it came to packing salt and firewood to distant places in the dry, hot desert.

Of course the stories of the camels continued to appear and to stir the curiosity of readers. An article appeared in the Virginia City, Nevada, *Territorial Enterprise* of March 14, 1863:

> THE CAMELS. The "ships of the desert" just arrived from the Walker River marshes, with a cargo of salt for the Central Mill, held a levee in this place and were visited by many curious and wondering bipeds. The venerable patriarch of the band did not seem to relish much the close attention of his visitors, and gave vent to his indignation and contempt by spitting at all who ventured near him. A coquettish old female who reclined at full length on the ground, screamed pettishly when some forward youngster attempted to toy with her shaggy locks. The camels appeared to be in good order.

The *Gold Hill News*[4] of April 16, 1864, had an interesting item, briefly entitled, "Plucking Camels." It read, "Yesterday, those in charge of the camels now stopping in Virginia[5] were engaged in plucking from their sides the heavy crop of wool which had accumulated during the winter. It was rather a painful operation, judging by the ludicrous faces these uncouth animals put on at each pluck, and the heartbroken bellowing that issued occasionally from the

---

[4] Gold Hill is part of the Comstock, just south of Virginia City.
[5] Refers to Virginia City.

cavernous depth of 'where they live.' " These certainly were the Bactrians Marius Chevalier had recently brought into Nevada.

Another item appeared on April 27, 1864. "At the dromedary race in Nevada, $9.50 was taken in admission and the show was compelled to pay $11 for a license. The profits of the race were of the left-handed order." (As has been noted before, the term "dromedary" was often used to refer to both species of camels, the one-hump and two-hump varieties.)

Not long after this we learn for the first time that the Chevalier people had taken a few of their camels to Austin.[6] The *Reese River Reveille*[7] heralded on August 26, 1864: "Ships of the Desert. A train of Bactrian camels arrived in town yesterday with a load of goods from the west. A large crowd soon gathered around the ugly beasts and curiously followed them to their place of unloading cargo. They carry immense loads and are hideous enough to frighten the natives out of the country."

A month after the arrival of the first camel train in Austin, the paper published this dispatch from a correspondent in Star City,[8] the only town between Boise Valley and Virginia City in 1864. The intervening distance consisted of 275 miles of sagebrush desert and high mountain ranges. It was bridged by a trail opened by Peter Ogden in 1828-29. According to Stanley Paher,

> . . . Star City with 1200 residents was the country's largest town and a place of busy enterprise with two hotels, one costing

---

[6] Austin, Nevada, high on the Toiyabe Range and almost the dead center of Nevada. The old Pony Express route passed a few miles south.

[7] The *Reese River Reveille* is still published in Austin.

[8] No vestige of Star City remains today. The town was 12 miles south of the Humboldt River and about halfway between present-day Lovelock and Winnemucca, Nevada.

$40,000, saloons, stores, Wells Fargo office, livery stables, post office, school, Sunday school with services conducted every other week by the Methodist minister, and a telegraph office with a special line to Virginia City . . . Star City shone brightest in 1864-65, when seven large mining companies conducted operations, and the town enjoyed such an amenity as a literary society known as the Gander Club, besides the usual pastimes and problems. It continued to be the scene of enthusiastic and productive mining and lively prospecting until 1868, but a swift turn from hope and prosperity to abandonment and despair resulted when ore at the Sheba mine ran out." [9]

When the first camel caravan arrived, the newspaper reported that ten of the animals were carrying almost 600 pounds apiece. "They were attended by a native Arabian from the south of Ireland," described as "having red hair and smoking a pipe." The camels were surely Chevalier's Bactrians from Dayton, Nevada.[10] On the second arrival of a caravan, the *Reveille* noted on September 28th: "Yesterday, our citizens were again visited by the 'ships of the desert,' loaded with castings for one of our quartz mills. Four of them were bearers of burden, and four more, in the infantile class, were too young to be put under the pack. One could almost imagine himself in the East, among the hills of Judea, climbing the Lybian mountains, when he looked upon these patient animals, with their long, awkward gait, striding through the streets."

On March 1, 1866, the *Reveille* reported in Austin:

Yesterday afternoon a train of camels – single and double humped – arrived in town from Virginia City, loaded with merchandise for the house of Albert Mau.[11] Although not heavily laden they were thirteen days making the trip from

---

[9] Stanley W. Paher, *Nevada Ghost Towns and Mining Camps* (Howell-North Books, Berkeley, Ca., 1970), pp. 135-36.

[10] Dayton is 12 miles south of Virginia City.

[11] In the 1861 *Directory of Nevada* it states that Albert Mau was a grocer on the east side of B street, opposite the post office in Virginia City.

Virginia. The whole weight of their cargo was 5,500 pounds – the greatest load carried by one animal being 700 pounds. There were twelve camels in the train, half of the number being mere youngsters, who were packed with light loads of fifty or sixty pounds. Most of the animals had their feet, made tender by the snow, bound in leather to protect them from the stony ground.

Again, on September 10th in the *Reveille:* "Camel Train. Our hump-backed friends, the camels, arrived in town this morning loaded with about 7,000 pounds of freight for the house of A. Mau. There were several youngsters in the train who have their first burden, and that a very light one. The animal is not ornamental, but apparently useful."

Many of the stories of the camels concern more than just reports of arrivals and departures. There are more personal stories as well. One of the best is about the camel driver, Hi Jolly, and Joe Plato. Hi Jolly was hauling granite for the construction of a mansion for Sandy Bowers, a Nevada Nabob. The Bowers claim was adjoined by a ten-foot claim belonging to Joe Plato, who met Hi Jolly as he carted the granite on Old Tuili and Maya,[12] two Bactrians. One day it suddenly occurred to Joe that he had only half his claim left, and he could not remember what he had done

---

[12] "The connection between the Bactrian male and the Arvana or female Arabian, produces a cross called 'Tulu,' generally known as the 'Turcoman' camel, large numbers of which are to be found throughout Asia Minor, and large caravans of them go annually from Smyrna to Persia . . . carrying immense loads. The cross or 'Tulu' is a hybrid and if it does produce at all, the issue is very small and inferior; it is called 'kokurt'; they are not worth five dollars." Arthur Woodward, *Camels and Surveyors in Death Valley* (Desert Printers, Inc., Palm Desert, Ca., 1961), pp. 12-13.

'Tulu' was also spelled 'Tuilu.' According to U.S. Secretary of War David Porter, in a letter written to Jefferson Davis, "The Maya, or female issue of the Bactrian male and Arabian female, is a very powerful animal, but cannot carry such heavy weights as the "Tulu." Woodward says that "Touli, or Trola, Maya and Catchouk were not proper names at all, but were the names applied to breeds of camels."

with five feet of his bonanza. Then he remembered!
During one glorious bacchanalian night in a gilded
palace on DuPont Street in San Francisco, he had
given five feet of claim to a beautiful woman as a
token of esteem. It was worth hundreds of thousands
of dollars. He had to get to San Francisco before the
lady knew what she had.

It was winter, and Joe had to cross the Sierra. With
a stroke of brilliance, he thought of Hi Jolly and the
camels. The camel driver agreed to go, and the two
set out through the snowdrifts. When they arrived in
San Francisco, it was too late. The lady knew what
she had and she told Joe that only a trip to the altar
would regain his claim. All three of them rode the
two camels back to Washoe, and, much to their relief,
found the ten precious feet still there, the claim un-
jumped under a blanket of snow.

In October of 1868, Judge A. W. Baldwin [13] and
General H. Williams [14] left Virginia City for Buckland's Station [15] to hold a political discussion. They
were traveling the Carson River road toward Fort
Churchill when they passed the Chevalier Ranch.
By that year, the Frenchman had discontinued his
trips to Virginia City and the camels were allowed
to graze in the open pastures and alongside the road.
They so frightened the team of horses the men were
driving that the horses ran away in panic, with the
coach careening crazily between the overhanging cliff
on one side and the Carson River on the other, and the

---

[13] U.S. District Judge A. W. Baldwin had been active in Nevada's Con-
stitutional Convention in 1863. As a dissident, he and William M. Stewart
bolted their party. Baldwin was later killed in a California railroad accident.

[14] Thomas H. Williams was a Democrat who ran for Senate in 1874 and
was defeated by Republican William Sharon.

[15] Buckland's Station was a Pony Express stop 1.3 miles east of Fort
Churchill. The Fort was not a change stop. Buckland's was on the Carson
River where the Pony Express forded.

two dismayed men holding on for their lives. It took about a mile of desperate struggle to regain control of the horses.

Not everyone had the attitude the judge and general and assorted packers developed towards Chevalier's camels. Louis Chevalier, who had been in the French army, had acquired a certain affection for camels. Without realizing it, he passed that affection on, at least to one segment of the population. Douglas McDonald gives this version:

> The quiet little mill town of Dayton in the 1860's offered little excitement to the eyes of its children. Millions in gold and silver passed them on the way down from the Comstock to be milled and refined, yet to them it was nothing unusual. But there was one thing they looked forward to eagerly – the day the camels came to town.
>
> Late in the afternoon, some school child would hear the faint tinkling of a camel bell or see far out on the Twenty-Six Mile Desert the long dusty column of camels. As soon as he had made sure what they were, he was off and running, crying "The camels are coming! The camels are coming!"
>
> The news spread like wildfire and by the time the camels had reached the outskirts of town and the special corrals built there, a large crowd of both children and adults had gathered . . .
>
> It took two days for a camel train to travel from Chevalier's ranch to Virginia City. The evening of the first day was the time all the children of Dayton looked forward to the time the camels came to town.[16]

It is difficult to reconcile the statement that Chevalier kept thirty camels on his ranch in the early years. It has been noted that Bactrians were already carrying salt in 1862 and 1864, and that at least eighteen of them were in use, except in 1868, when they were seen grazing at his ranch.

As indicated in *Camels to California,* Greenwood

---

[16] Douglas McDonald, "The Camels are Coming," *The West* (Feb., 1967).

and Company took ten of Uncle Sam's camels from Marysville [17] to Nevada in 1864, and McLeneghan took twelve more in 1865, for a total of twenty-two. McLeneghan owned a fenced corral in Dayton, built by George Leslie. The camels were apparently in the care of LaFlamme, McLeneghan's half-brother. The beasts were driven to Yuma, California, in 1865, but now it appears that it was 1866 when they crossed the Colorado River into Arizona. Within this short period of time probably half a dozen calves were born.

A news item in Virginia City, Montana Territory, on June 3, 1865, noted that seven camels had arrived. McLeneghan's twenty-two dromedaries and the remainder of Esche's Bactrians from San Francisco, also twenty-two in number, were corraled at Dayton on that date. Therefore, the seven seen in Montana Territory certainly came from Laumeister's old caravan.

But the Bactrians were still being used on the Comstock, as the *Territorial Enterprise* related on May 15, 1869. "The Camel Nuisance. The camels have made their reappearance on the Carson River, more numerous than ever; and again the lives and limbs of the traveling public along that route are to be endangered." The *Enterprise* was to become a strong advocate of the abolishment of the camels from the roads of Nevada.

Up to 1869, the growth of the Bactrians' young ones must have been substantial, and could well have reached a total of thirty animals. The adults had been on Chevalier's ranch for eight years. This is partially confirmed in the item from the Los Angeles *Daily News,* September 25, 1870.

Herd of 25 camels on a ranch on Carson River in Nevada

---

[17] On the Yuba River in northern California, across from Yuba.

8 miles below the mouth of Six Mile Canyon. All but two are native born in the United States. Only two of the original nine or ten beasts first brought into Nevada some years ago, now living. Original camels fell to Mexican hands who did not know how to handle them. Present owners are Frenchmen. Animals used to pack salt from marshes in the desert 60 miles to eastward. Beasts eat all sorts of desert vegetation. Strongest animal can carry 1100 pounds.

It appears camels were also used in the Genoa area. Long, narrow hames found in a Genoa stockyard were first thought to have been used on oxen, but later investigations showed camel hairs on the pads of the hames. A hame is one of two curved pieces of wood in the type of harness adapted for heavy draft animals, to which the traces are fastened. This would indicate that Bactrians, possibly young ones, were used to haul heavy wagons loaded with supplies or ore, a service rendered by oxen.

There is still a mystery as to why McCleneghan remained such a short time in Dayton in 1865 and then went on to Yuma, where he died about 1866. It may be that, after 1862, Chevalier had secured a monopoly by carrying salt in sufficient quantities from Sand Springs to Virginia City, supplying the needs of the mills. As mentioned earlier, the Chinese were heavily involved in the wood trade and may have had the field to themselves. There were reports that McLeneghan's camels were used at Austin, carrying salt from the Columbus Salt Marsh, but this is doubtful.

Seeing that it was not possible to meet the competition, perhaps McLeneghan made a desperate decision to go to Arizona. He may have taken the old Indian Trail (Highway 395) to San Bernardino, a distance of about 425 miles. Here he would have lingered, remembering the time he was with Greek George and

Hi Jolly on Edward Beale's camel expedition. He
may have been thinking of the time they rode their
camels into Los Angeles on that memorable November
9th in 1857.

He would then have gone south forty miles to Te-
mecula where he picked up the old Butterfield Stage
Road to Warner's Ranch, Vallecito Station, Coyote
Wells, Cookes Wells, and Yuma, a distance of about
225 miles.

It was chaparral country from San Bernardino to
a few miles past Warner's Ranch. The remainder of
the route traversed desert, where there was little water,
high mountains, and eroded country subject to high
winds and dust storms, lightning and severe cloud-
bursts. It was enough to scare the wits out of the most
hardened dromedary. Outside of San Bernardino, the
passage would have taken five weeks and covered 700
miles at a leisurely pace of twenty miles a day.

Another reason why McLeneghan left Nevada was
because the Comstock Lode was running out. The production decreased by almost half between 1867 and
1869. In all parts of the world, the richest silver ores
are to be found within a few hundred feet of the surface, and by 1869 the biggest bonanzas were nearly
exhausted. The Ophir had failed; the Gould and
Curry body were almost gone; the Yellow Jacket was
nearly played out. It is little wonder the camels were
led away. There was no more for them to do.

5

Frank Laumeister in Nevada

Frank Laumeister's biography tells us "he was leaving Victoria on the *Wright,* presumably to take up residence in the United States in 1868." It then goes on to relate that he was at Elko, Nevada, in 1869, "interested in the currency of the country," and was a real estate agent. A son Charley was mentioned as being at Elko with his father. Laumeister was still at Elko in December, 1870, where he owned real estate and had "chicken-soup springs."

In the *Elko Independent* of May 21, 1870, Elko County Librarian Mrs. Ruth Hoskins gives us a confirmation of his presence, when she mentions a letter written by a German traveler: "F. W. Laumeister, who with a Mr. Groepper has erected a very comodious bathing house at the Hot Springs in Elko."

It appears there were advertisements in every issue before this time about the Humboldt Sulphur Springs bath house run by Laumeister and Groepper. Then in a later issue for November 9, 1870, the paper mentions that "F. W. Laumeister had disposed of his interest in the Humboldt Sulphur Springs."

This explains the ambiguous meaning of "chicken soup springs," and the fact that the real estate was a bath house. However, there was still no word of the camels.

This is indeed startling news, and requires some discussion. Laumeister undoubtedly arrived in San

Francisco about July 1, 1868, and spent the time traveling around the country until about April 1, 1869.

The Central Pacific Railroad was nearing the linking with the Union Pacific Railroad at Promontory, near the northern end of the Great Salt Lake. The linking was at least consummated on the afternoon of May 10, 1869, and created the dawn of a new way of life and new avenues of commercial exploitation. The Central Pacific had already passed Elko when Laumeister had arrived there. But long before that the Emigrant Trail between Salt Lake City and Genoa, Nevada, passed through that area (1848). Why Elko? In 1867-68, gold and silver were being discovered north of Elko in Tuscarora, Mountain City, and Columbia, and south of Elko, in Bullion City, Treasure City, and other places. So rapidly did these towns grow that every means of transporting food, goods, and freight was brought into play, just as they were at a similar stage of development in Idaho and Montana. The source of supply was at Elko where the Central Pacific Railroad was deluged with demand for goods. Most of the food, lumber, and feed for animals came from the Sacramento Valley; machinery for the new mills and clothing came from San Francisco.

Laumeister must have been surprised with the developments around the Bay area, and certainly spent some time in Carson City where a new bonanza of silver deposits was being opened. There he interviewed the Chevalier people about the operation of their Bactrian pack trains which had also originated from Esche's forty-five camels. He possibly visited Austin which was then nearing its zenith of gold and silver production.

All these expanding mining operations with promise

of great wealth apparently did not appeal to Laumeister, who had recently seen the hazard of mining in the Cariboo. He also learned that freighting by means of camels was not as profitable as it was in British Columbia.

Now we find him in Elko. There must have been some other incentive for him to move there besides land investments. It has already been recorded that the Bactrians were packing into Idaho's Boise Valley, and possibly into Bannock, Idaho, and Virginia City, Montana, via the Oregon Trail.

How these animals were used in that part of the country at that late date is still unknown, but it is likely that Laumeister kept in close communication with their packers.

In all the ramifications relating to the camel episode, we do not know who any of the owners or the drivers were. Surely camels do not travel by themselves in strange lands among strange people. But there it is, always the camels here, the camels there, the excitement of people seeing them. Who took loving care of them in the severe winters, and who housed them? No one knows, or at least it is not recorded.

At any rate there is unmistakable evidence that Laumeister came into possession of his long abandoned Bactrians. They could have come by way of the Glenn Ferry Crossing[1] over the Snake River or by the old Fort Hall trading post, also on the Snake River, then via the California Trail across the sagebrush desert, past Halleck Station[2] to Elko.

But where were these Bactrians kept since our last recorded date of 1867 to 1869, and who took care of them? This writer believes they wandered free in the

---

[1] Located in southwestern Idaho.

[2] Twenty miles east of Elko, on the Central Pacific Railroad route.

open desert of northern Nevada, and that their presence was related to Laumeister by emigrants and miners crossing that area. Laumeister most likely sent men out to bring the camels to some isolated area near Elko where he could corral them, so they could not cause any more expensive stampedes among the horses and mules.

And, as usual, the cost of freighting northwest from Elko to Tuscarora, fifty-two miles over high mountains and deserts, was so expensive that everybody's jackass got into the act. Freight also had to be delivered to Columbia (sixty-seven miles) and Mountain City (eighty-four miles), both due north of Elko. Likewise, there was great demand for supplies to Bullion City (twenty-seven miles) and to Treasure City (125 miles), which had 6000 people. Both were south of Elko.

No doubt Laumeister was tempted to put his trained Bactrians to work to earn a good income while he invested in real estate. The town of Elko grew by leaps and bounds, and provided substantial revenues for land speculators.

Mrs. Frank Leslie and her husband, of the famous *Leslie Illustrated Magazine* of New York City, made a trip to the Southwest about 1877. In her diary, she records staying over a few days in Elko, which was the first Nevada town they came to, after leaving Salt Lake City. There they refreshed themselves from the hot ride across the Salt Lake and deserts, for Elko boasted of six hot and cold mineral springs, one of which "is agreeably known as the Chicken Soup Spring and requires only pepper and salt and a willing imagination to make it a perpetual free soup kitchen. A bathhouse is already erected and a large hotel is to follow, which is confidently expected will bring fashion and civilization by the carload into Elko." This is further clarification of the ambiguous meaning of "chicken soup springs," and it seems to confirm that Laumeister's bathhouse was a reality.

Laumeister's biography then records that he was at Pioche, Nevada, in 1872. Pioche, 250 miles southeast of Elko, began with a silver discovery in the winter of 1863-64, but it was not until 1870 that production amounted to over $600,000. The nearest Central Pacific station was 275 miles north, so large freight wagons were required to haul supplies and mining machinery to this isolated camp.

Business and population grew with increasing shipments of bullion. Several dozen saloons thrived, as well as a flourishing red-light district, in this town of over 7,000 restless souls. During 1871, real estate values rose handsomely, and lots formerly worth $100 or less sold in the thousands. Perhaps it was this upsurge of real estate value that brought Laumeister to Pioche.

But he must have been shocked by the lawlessness of the town, for law enforcement was ineffective in this remote place, and most offenses generally went unpunished. The frequency of homicide alone made Pioche notorious for gunplay. Nearly sixty percent of Nevada's killing reported in 1871 and 1872 occurred in the Pioche area.

During the early years, excessive claim-jumping, fraud, and killing made guns the only law, and "reliable legends" insists that violent deaths accounted for over six dozen graves in Boot Hill before a citizen of Pioche succumbed to natural causes. The dead were buried with their boots on, and some men dug their own graves before being shot.

Laumeister apparently did not stay very long in

Pioche. Perhaps his Bactrians were causing stampedes on the trail, and pistol-packing packers were threatening not only the camels, but Laumeister, too.

Something serious like this must have happened to cause him to leave soon after his arrival, and go so far away. According to Roscoe Willson, "we find one Horace Winter quoted in an eastern paper as having seen 50 camels unloaded from a steamer at Yuma,[3] in 1872, and driven through the streets by Hi Jolly. I can find no substantiation of this story." However, there must be some element of truth to part of it, though it has been garbled through the years, for at least thirty of these fifty camels must have belonged to Laumeister.

For these animals to have been shipped down the Colorado River, Laumeister would have taken the trail southwest to Hiko, then south past the Mormon settlement at Alamo to the Las Vegas Mission,[4] the crossroads on the old Spanish Trail between southern Utah and San Bernardino. They then continued southeast to Eldorado[5] where local legend claims the district had been mined for over 150 years by Indians, Spanish explorers, and occasional Mormon emigrants.

Laumeister's caravan was now 200 miles from Pioche, going by dubious roads through treacherous terrain where Indians and robbers lurked. Not even a killing was sufficient reason for authorities to come; the locals formed their own posses and vigilante groups to capture and punish wrongdoers.

It could take as long as six months for supplies to come from San Francisco; flatbottom steamers carried

---

[3] Yuma, Arizona.

[4] Las Vegas Mission was the original Mormon settlement in the area.

[5] Eldorado is near the southern tip of Nevada on the west side of the Eldorado Range, which cuts the settlement off from the Colorado River to the east. The town is now called Nelson, and is twenty miles southeast of Searchlight, Nevada. One hundred years ago the spelling was El Dorado.

the cargo the last leg of the journey from Yuma, Arizona, and often more than a month passed between steamer visits to Fort Mohave, some forty miles south of Eldorado, and 180 miles from Yuma.

In view of the norotious killing and robbery in that desolate desert country and probably upon the advice of the army officers at Fort Mohave, Laumeister arranged with a steamer captain to take his camels on board the vessel and steam down the Colorado River to Yuma. Laumeister, his drivers, and the Bactrians might never have reached Yuma, had he continued traveling the desert roads which paralleled the river.

The coincidence of Laumeister's being in Pioche in 1872 and the reported arrival of fifty camels by steamer at Yuma in 1872 strengthens the conclusion that this was Laumeister's caravan. We will have more to add about it later on.

Perhaps Laumeister saw what was coming: a movement to ban camels from Nevada's roads. It was the usual problems – camels stampeded the pack trains.

Ever since the Mayor of Virginia City failed to approve the town fathers' ordinance prohibiting camels in that town, there was continued pressure by irate teamsters until the Nevada legislators finally acted.

A February 4, 1875 letter written to the *Reveille* from correspondent Van Jaquelin in Carson City, appeared in the Austin paper on February 8th. It indicated that the august Nevada Senate was debating somewhat ribaldly on an anti-camel bill introduced in the Assembly.

> The Senate devoted a large portion of the morning session to a little fun over the Assembly bill to prohibit camels from traveling public roads and highways in this state. A motion was made for its reference to the Committee on Public Morals, to which an amendment was offered that it be to the Com-

mittee on Indian Affairs. A discussion ensued, in which some jokes were cracked about humps in general, and, finally a substitute that the bill be referred to the Lyon and Churchill delegation.

Humorous or not, the bill was eventually passed and noted, Seventh Session, Laws of Nevada, page 53, Chapter XII, Approved February 9th, 1875 read:

An act to prohibit camels and dromedaries from running at large on or about the public highways of the State of Nevada.

The People of Nevada represented in Senate and Assembly, do enact as follows:

Section 1. From and after the passage of this Act it shall be unlawful for the owner or owners of any camel or camels, dromedary or dromedaries, to permit them to run at large on or about the public roads or highways of this State.

Section 2. If any owner or owners of any camel or camels, dromedary or dromedaries, shall, knowingly or wilfully permit any violation of this Act, he or they shall be deemed guilty of a misdemeanor and shall be arrested, on complaint of any person feeling aggrieved; and when convicted, before any Justice of the Peace, he or they shall be punished by a fine of not less than twenty-five (25) or more than one hundred (100) dollars, or by imprisonment of not less than ten or more than thirty days, or by both such fine and imprisonment.

The faithful Reese River *Reveille,* which kept an eagle eye on everything that happened within the State of Nevada, reported September 25, 1875:

THOSE DROMEDARIES

The first prosecution under the Legislature Act prohibiting dromedaries from running at large in the state of Nevada, came up in Judge Hickley's justice court at Dayton, on Monday and was postponed for hearing till today at 2 p.m. Like the poor 'droms' the citizens of Walker River Valley have got their backs up and want the unsightly animals properly restrained. Nothing is safe from these voracious critters, as they will bolt down a Murphy wagon, four rods of rail fence, a Yankee stone boat or anything else at a single meal. As pack animals for use across a desert waste they can't be beat, but when it comes to a bump of destructiveness they have one as big as a Brooklyn preacher.

The *Territorial Enterprise* of May 10, 1876, stated "A camel train loaded with wood came into town night before last, freighting along B Street. Each camel carried half a cord of wood. Some emigrants who happened to see the train considered it the event of their lives."

Apparently an exception was made to circumvent this new law, for according to Douglas McDonald we may quote the following:

The Fourth of July, 1876, was the nation's centennial and Virginia City decided to have a celebration worthy of the name. One of the attractions was Mt. Davidson, which would be visible in all the surrounding valleys. Since the slopes were practically barren of wood, camels were hired to carry it up. Early on the morning of June 28, eight camels, carrying a third of a cord of wood apiece, started up the steep mountain. That afternoon, they were unloaded 150 from the summit and started back down. The next morning, the rest of the firewood was carried up and a far-sighted reporter on the *Territorial Enterprise* wrote how unfortunate it was that there was no photographer in town to record the unusual sight.

In the Fall of 1876, Virginia City councilmen drafted an ordinance prohibiting camels from entering the city limits during the day. The Mayor refused to pass it claiming that camels had just as much right on Virginia City streets as anyone else did. But with the arrival of the Virginia and Truckee Railroad, the need for camel transportation . . . was over.[6]

Although Mt. Davidson is about 7,800 feet in elevation, the valley surrounding Dayton is close to 6,000 feet – thus the actual climbing height was only 1,800 feet, and the exertion on the camels was not severe. Furthermore, these animals were all young ones raised at Chevalier's ranch.

[6] "The Camels are Coming," Douglas B. McDonald, *The West* (Maverick Pubs., Inc., Freeport, N.Y.), p. 34.

Apparently this new law was still being defied, for the *Territorial Enterprise* of October 31, 1876, noted, "A train of twenty camels loaded with wood, came into town about eleven o'clock last night. On account of their frightening horses and mules they are not allowed to enter town during daylight."

The *Goldfield News* of Goldfield, Nevada, in their 23rd December, 1904 issue, had this to say:

> The following, which probably originated in the fertile imagination of a 'space filler,' is now being extensively copied by the State press:
> "Before long the old scriptural camel will be used to carry provisions along the desert to Goldfield. A company has been formed to capture camels which abound near here and utilize them. They are the ones used years ago in Virginia City. The herd escaped and has multiplied, and many hundreds are now roaming the deserts of Nye and Esmeralda counties."

Again, the same paper of September 8, 1905:

THOSE LOST CAMELS

> Last Wednesday a party of prospectors arrived at Stephanite and reported they had seen a herd of sixteen camels about five miles east of here, says the *Silver Bow Standard*. In the herd were fourteen old ones and two young ones. They had just come in off the desert and were going for water.
>
> The gentlemen attempted to follow the animals but their horses would not go near the beasts.
>
> This is probably the herd that used to pack ore from the Comstock mines in early days and were turned loose, or those used by the Southern Pacific in building its road in Arizona. They have not been seen for several years and it is an interesting fact to know that they are breeding on our desert.

What happened to those free roamers of the desert is not known, but the Arizona camels take us to our last chapters.

6

The Arizona Sequel

It would appear from *Camels to California* that the end of the trail for Uncle Sam's camels under Samuel McLeneghan was reached at Fort Yuma, Arizona, in 1866. Shortly after arrival he became ill and died, leaving his half-brother LaFlamme, Hi Jolly, and Greek George stranded there on their own resources.

His herd of between twenty-five and thirty camels was the parent stock of the so-called wild camels that roamed at large over the southwestern corner of the Arizona desert from that year until shortly after the turn of the century.

For a while Hi Jolly, and probably LaFlamme, stayed in Yuma to keep the camels corralled until they could be put to use. Greek George returned to Los Angeles, and became a naturalized citizen by the name of George Allen.

For a time Hi Jolly contracted to haul freight from Fort Yuma to Tucson and to California desert points, as supplies of all kinds arrived on regularly scheduled steamers from Los Angeles. He also used the camels for a short time between San Diego and El Paso.

The following stories are from Roscoe Willson's [1] articles: "Uncle Billy" Fourr, who operated stage stations between Yuma and Gila Bend during the 1860s, recalled that for a short time "a little Arab" used to come by with about twenty-five camels loaded

---

[1] Roscoe G. Willson, "Camels in Arizona and the West," *Arizona Republic* (March 6-April 4, 1966), Phoenix, Ariz.

with water, which he sold to travelers along the desert road. Fourr built a toll road near his Oatman Flat stage station in 1868 and the Arab came over it with his camels and, shortly thereafter, turned them loose along the river. Fourr also related he had four or five of them in his corral at one time, but that they got loose and rambled off.

We cannot doubt the statement of Tom Childs [2] that his father used to kill a camel occasionally in the 1870s and even later for the meat and grease the carcass contained. Childs said in a letter to Willson, dated October 14, 1948:

> I don't know of anyone who may have a picture of these camels. They were quite plentiful all along the Gila River in the late 60's and '70's and then all seemed to vanish about 1892. The lost one I heard of was caught by Denney Matigan near Enterprise Ranch (just below Gillespie Dam).[3] People came to look at it and in showing it off he was kicked by it and laid up. He turned it loose. There would still be lots of them if the Papago Indians had not found out they were good eating. Old Man Daniel Noonan of Gila Bend killed quite a few of them and made jerkey of them.
>
> Old Man High Jolly, the Arab that helped bring them to this country, came here to Ajo in 1888 or '89 to try to catch some to prospect with. Some of these camels reached as far down as the Gulf of California, but they were easy prey for the Papagos. They were all gentle and easy to get up to.
>
> High Jolly lived at my home in Ajo and used to tell me stories of his travels with the camels to and from El Paso to San Diego (with the short lived camel express) and of some of the races he won against horses.

It has been related before that Frank Laumeister was briefly in Pioche in 1872; and that another source

---

[2] Tom Childs owned a ranch near Ajo, Arizona, and lived with a Papago wife and many children and Papago relatives. He owned a large part of New Cornelia copper mine, later sold to Phelps-Dodge for $90,000.

[3] Gillespie Dam is on the Gila River, about thirty miles north of Gila Bend, Arizona.

indicated that camels were seen in Yuma being landed from a steamer.

But what became of Laumeister's beloved Bactrians?

In an interview with a Tombstone *Epitaph* reporter in 1883, an old timer said the camels were brought to Arizona from Nevada to pack from the Silver King mine to Yuma in 1873. There must be an error in dating here, as the discovery of the rich silver mine near Superior was first made in 1875, and the mine itself was probably not in operation until 1876-77. The old timer's citing of 1873 may be the correct date for the camels' arrival, but it was certainly before the time of the Silver King mine.

However, the first gold rush in Arizona did start in 1858, when rich placers were found near the Colorado River at Gila City. A few years later the placer mines at La Paz and Ehrenberg in Yuma County were discovered, and at the same time placer fields were found in central Arizona, at Rich Hill, Lynx Creek and Hassayampa in the Bradshaw Mountains. It is not known whether the Bactrians were used in any of these places.

Nell Murbarger tells us that Silver King [4] and Pinal City [5] had their beginning in the days of Apache warfare, when any man foolhardy enough to venture alone into the mountains of Arizona Territory was lucky to keep his scalp, whether or not he discovered a mine.

As an aid in combatting Apache depredations, General George Stoneman established Camp Picketpost. Here, in 1872, he began construction of a road leading into the more inaccessible portion of the Pinals.

In 1874, a prospecting party headed by Charles G.

---

[4] Silver King mine was discovered in 1876 near Superior, Arizona. Silver King was also the name of a small settlement near the mine.

[5] Pinal City was the milling town for the Silver King mine.

Mason located the Globe mine. The following spring, Mason and four of his friends took a train of pack animals to the Globe location with the idea of bringing out a shipment of ore. While returning from the mine, March 21, 1875, this party was attacked by Apaches and one of its members was slain. Soon after completion of the simple obsequy, the four surviving members made camp and Isaac Copeland went to bring back one of their mules which had strayed. When he found the animal standing on some croppings he paused to examine them. Moments later, he came rushing back to camp shouting, "I have struck it!"

Gathering around Copeland, the excited and hopeful prospectors passed the pieces of croppings from hand to hand and all agreed that this was the same black silver ore that a miner named Sullivan had found three years earlier. The Silver King location was discovered the following day, and two weeks later, on April 3, 1875, the *Arizona Citizen* reported:

> Pinal County stands ahead now in the matter of a silver deposit, according to all accounts. The discovery is about 32 miles by trail from Florence, at the foot of Stoneman Grade. It consists of a deposit of ore worth thousands of dollars per ton; in fact, some pieces of pure silver weighing pounds are said to have been found . . . Mr. Reagan . . . brought a ton of the ore to town, a sample of which was assayed here showing it worth $4,340 per ton . . .

Convinced that the mine was "too good to last," Copeland and Long soon sold to Mason and Reagan for $80,000 each, and in January, 1877, Mason sold his half interest to Colonel James M. Barney, of Yuma, for a quarter of a million dollars.

Despite the dire predictions of sundry calamity-howlers, news from the King continued to be good. "Two trains, one drawn by 18 and the other by 20 mules, bringing 36,050 pounds of rich silver ore from the famous Silver King mine of Arizona, arrived in town yesterday," reported the San Diego *Union,* January 19, 1877. "This ore is consigned to W. W. Stewart & Co., by Colonel Barney, and will be forwarded to San Francisco for reduction.

The San Francisco *Stock Report* of April 30, 1877, listed a sale of thirty-three tons of Silver King ore, the best of which brought $4,650 per ton, and the lowest grade $1,230. Two months later (June 30, 1877) the *Arizona Citizen* noted that the Silver King had been shipping thirty tons of silver ore per month for about a year, with no ore being shipped that yielded less than $1,000 per ton.

Benjamin W. Reagan, the last remaining owner of the four original locaters, sold his half interest in the mine in May, 1877, for a reported $300,000. The Silver King Mining Company, organized in San Francisco that summer, was capitalized at $10,000,000, and James M. Barney was named as manager. Thus we know for a fact that the Silver King mine was fabulous.

Roscoe Willson notes that the Florence, Arizona, newspaper reported two Frenchmen passing through in 1876 with thirty camels, bound for Sonora, Mexico.[6]

In *Camels and Survivors in Death Valley,* Woodward states that a John B. Hart, who had lived in Florence, Pinal County, in July, 1877, said "we saw the two Frenchmen with their bunch of 28 camels – we counted them – passing along the main street of Florence headed southward. We inquired of the Frenchmen about their destination and was told it was a mining camp in Sonora but do not remember the name of it."

---

[6] Willson, "Camels in Arizona and the West."

Charles M. Clark, who claimed he was a military telegraph operator in the office at Florence in 1876, gave some of his reminiscences to the Arizona *Republican* April 10, 1929, and said that the camels were brought to that point to transport silver ore from the Silver King mine to an adobe smelter owned by a man by the name of Jennings in Florence. He also said that the camel train made one of two trips into town from the mine, but that the animals couldn't stand the rigors of crossing the Arizona mountain terrain. The camels themselves were driven down along the Gila River west of Florence, where they roamed at large for a number of years. Clark said there were about forty animals in that bunch.

Thus we have three versions of the camels' presence in Florence, with two mentioning the two Frenchmen, who could have been either Laumeister and his son Charley, or the Chevaliers, and the third claiming that the camels were owned by two Greeks, one of whom was Hi Jolly. Two of the accounts also mentioned that the animals were being taken to Sonora in 1876-77.

The real puzzle, however, is what was happening to Laumeister's caravan between 1872 and 1877. It is difficult to believe that the camels were kept idle all those years. We may have an answer to this question but it does confuse the chronology of events, and does not clear up the missing years in question, unless the dating is in error.

Woodward gives the following: The Prescott *Courier* of June 3, 1911, reprinting an item from the *Observer,* under the title "Those Camels Again," quoted the writer for the *Observer* –

In the year 1876, two Frenchmen gathered together the loose camels then roaming over the desert section north of the Salt and

Gila rivers, numbering some thirty-odd heads. These camels were taken to Nevada for the purpose of packing wood and salt into the Comstock mines. My old pard Johnny Hart . . . went up to Virginia City atop one of the huge beasts. The Nevada country was too stony for the soft-footed camels and furthermore these ungainly animals so frightened the freighters' mules and were such a nuisance the old Comstock freighters notified the Frenchmen to take the camels out of that country or else the camels would be shot; as it was three or four were shot and killed by the Nevada teamsters.

The Frenchmen started south with their camels; their objective point being a mining camp in Sonora, Mexico. John Hart also returned to Arizona along with the camels.

There is another angle to this that may confirm its truthfulness, except for the dating. When Laumeister found there were no means of putting his Bactrians to work, he probably did return to survey the situation, by way of the Butterfield Stage Route taken by McCleneghan.

So this was the end of "Laumeister's Folly" – or was it?

Joseph Miller [7] quotes an item from the Tombstone *Epitaph* of August 25, 1883: "The *Epitaph* received a pleasant call yesterday from Philip Tedro, who is known throughout the Territory as Hi Jolly. He announced he had just returned from Sonora where he was in the employ of the San Augustin Mining Company. A sketch of his career will not prove uninteresting."

Is it possible that this was the mine to which the Bactrians were being taken out of Florence in 1876-77?

Now we have the final reading of Frank Laumeister's life. His obituary reveals that he died at Yuma, Arizona, February 17, 1891, at the age of sixty-nine. He was survived by three daughters in British Columbia: Mrs. Steve Tingley (Pauline), Mrs. Arthur Stevenson

---

[7] Joseph Miller lived in Phoenix and was a prolific writer.

(Agnes – previously married to Thomas Russell Buie),
and Mrs. Isaac Van Volkenburgh (Christine). He was
also survived by two sons, both of whose whereabouts
were unknown.

One cannot help but wonder how Laumeister came
to live in Yuma, which did not have a savory reputation in those years, and which was so far away from
his home in British Columbia. Nevertheless, his end
came in this frontier desert town. According to Frank
Lockwood's *Pioneer Days in Arizona,* we find the
following:

> Yuma has had its ups and downs . . . In 1872 the levees on
> the Gila side gave way; in 1884 much damage was done to the
> bridge, and the streets were inundated; most destructive of all
> was the flood in February, 1891, when the Gila on two occasions,
> four days apart, poured its turbulent waters over the whole town,
> leaving only fifty buildings standing out of three hundred fifty.

It would appear from this narrative that Frank Laumeister was drowned in that flood of February, 1891.

One of Laumeister's obituaries stated that he arrived
at Yuma fourteen years before his death, or in 1877.
This was the year the camels were taken into Sonora.
But the frustrating part, insofar as this writer is concerned, is that neither of the two obituaries mention
his connection with the Bactrian episode in any shape
or form.

It has been told that the camel driver Elias, a Syrian
immigrant, went into Sonora, possibly with the Frenchmen, where he married a half Yaqui Indian woman
named Calles. They settled down on a little rancho
near Guaymas, Mexico, where a son Plutarco Elias
Calles was born July 20, 1877. He went to school in
Hermosillo, where, in his youth, he was known as "el
Turko" (the Turk). He was President of Mexico from
1924-1927. The family is named after the wife's sur-

name, Calles, in whom all property is vested under Mexican law.

We may also wonder what happened to Louis Chevalier's camels. The *Arizona Citizen* of February 26, 1876, printed the following:

THE CAMELS ARE COMING

The camels formerly used in packing salt to the Comstock mines, will shortly be taken to Arizona, for service in the desert of that country. Since the introduction of these animals into Nevada, some ten years ago, they have increased by breeding from eight to forty-two.

This prospective coming of the camels is very opportune. It is a shameful fact, probably not known to the world at large, that the great Territory of Arizona, with an area of 113,000 square miles, including standing room for the editor of the *Arizona Miner,* has not hitherto had a solitary herd of camels within its confines. At least the superintendent of Wells, Fargo & Co. doesn't make any mention of such an animal (the camel, not the editor of the *Miner*) in his late report. And he ought to know, because his company has offices in Oregon.

We are particularly glad that these animals are coming. Times are hard, and a good many people here and elsewhere, who hadn't anything to do when we first knew them, some four years ago, have more than ordinarily had nothing to do lately. They have been growing more and more bitter against fate and their fellows, as the pressure of hard times crowded them. But here will be something to do at last. They can look at these camels. Let their souls be glad once more. There shall be camels in the streets, with the natural pin-backs on; there shall be corners to stand at, and hands in pockets, and satisfied souls, and perchance music.

Up to this point we have been unable to differentiate between the Chevalier group of Bactrians with those of Laumeister's; the latter apparently came from the Boise Valley and left by way of Salt Lake for Nevada.

The first hint of the arrival of Chevalier's original band of Bactrians in Arizona was noted in the *San Diego Union,* March 17, 1877. It carried a succinct telegraphic communication headed: "Yuma: A drove

of camels arrived here today from California." Another drove of camels had arrived, the first since Mc-
Leneghan's eleven years before.

Let's read what the *Arizona Sentinel* (Yuma), of
March 17, 1877, said:

> The camels were interviewed by our reporter this week. Hearing
> they were camped on the other side of the river a few miles from
> the Fort, we hunted up a walled-eyed pinto horse, as being more
> like a circus horse and therefore less liable to scare at the sight
> of the strange animals, and started for the camp. The brush was
> thick and it began to look like a fruitless quest, when some tracks
> were seen about the size of a pie plate and soon after a *pungent,
> goatlike odor* announced the proximity of the camels. The horse
> had evidently not been in a circus for some time, for nothing
> could induce him to approach the strange beasts. There were
> thirty-six of them of all ages, sizes and of both sexes, the tallest
> one measuring about nine feet to the top of his hump and the
> smallest being no larger than a large calf.
>
> They were in charge of two Frenchmen who started from
> Nevada with forty-one head, but lost five on the road. Eight
> of the largest are said to be able to carry a load of one thousand
> pounds each. The owners have no definite plans, but are open
> to any engagement for transportation over desert roads. Camels
> cannot travel on wet ground; having no hoofs, their spongy
> feet soon give out and get sore when wet. This is the same lot
> that the government had at *Drum barracks a few years ago,*
> and a rough looking lot they are. *They are the color of a snuffy
> buffalo robe,* with awkward movement, ungainly shape and no
> redeeming feature, except the eye, which is indeed large, lus-
> trous, and lovely. Their gait is a long slow pace, both legs of one
> side being moved forward at the same time. To ride one any dis-
> tance requires great powers of endurance and "copper-bottomed"
> posteriors. They are perfectly docile, lying down and getting up
> at the word of command – accompanied by thumps and kicks.
> The Yuma Indians seem to express no wonder at them and act
> as if camels were what they were raised on.

The following seems to confirm that Chevalier's
caravan was on its way from Dayton, Nevada, to Arizona as reported in the Inyo *Register* of October 25,

1923, under the title of "Western Camels": "There may be Inyoites who recall seeing a herd of camels driven through Owens Valley (California), probably about 1877." This indicates the route was along the Old Indian Trail, now Highway 395.

Then on March 24, 1877, the *Sentinel* again notes:

THE CAMELS AGAIN

The camel pack train, which has been camped on the California side of the river below Fort Yuma, was brought in Friday last for pasturage on the Gila. In getting them over the ferry and in arranging their pack saddles, etc., they were put through all their evolutions of kneeling down etc., and attracted much attention. The owners had lost two of them on the California side of the river, and while looking for them had kept the rest of the herd tied up four days without feed, hence they looked somewhat gaunt. We have been asked to publish some information about camels and give all we have been able to cull from the limited sources within reach. A gentleman here who has seen thousands of them in Northern Africa says that the grown ones of this lot average much larger in size than those he saw there, and are covered with more and longer hair. Another one, who was formerly engaged with these camels in California, says that the oldest of them cannot be over ten years old now, the original ones having died off and all the others having been born in this country . . .

On April 7, 1877, the *Sentinel* again reports:

The owners of the camels can thank Mr. S. W. Simon of Ehrenberg for giving the following information to the SENTINEL; i.e., if it is of any use to them. One of the camels, lost by them near Ft. Yuma, was at Chuckawalla [8] with a young one on the 29th ult., and another was about 25 miles below Ehrenberg on the California bank of the Colorado river.

On May 19, 1877, the following appeared: "A camel strayed into town yesterday and we hear of others at Mission Camp, Maricopa [9] and various places.

---

[8] Chuckawalla was a small town a few miles west of Yuma.

[9] Mission Camp was east of Yuma near present-day Wellton, some thirty-five miles south from Yuma. Maricopa is south of Phoenix.

What has become of their keepers? The herd seems to be disorganized."

The November 9, 1878, issue mentions:

The arrival here of Romeo, Ryland's trained camel, reminds us that a camel is said to be running at large between here and Las Flores; his tracks are often seen on the bottoms along the river. Another, with a young one, is said to be roaming in the neighborhood of Chuckawalla. And still another was reported in the vicinity of Roods Ranch [10] a few months ago. They escaped from a herd that was brought into Arizona a year and a half ago.

The following letter is of interest:

Yuma, Arizona, Feb. 24, 1914

Mr. Merrill P. Freeman,
Tucson, Arizona.

My dear Mr. Freeman:

I arrived in Yuma in 1877. The Camels were here at that time and running loose up and down the Gila and Colorado rivers. Nearly every circus that came along would pay the Mexicans to bring them in. So that by this means they soon were all taken that could be caught. I do not think there is any left in Yuma County.

Sincerely yours,
Geo. W. Norton

The *Arizona Sentinel* (Yuma) of February 1, 1879, reports:

A herd of camels was driven here from Nevada, nearly two years ago. Finding no profitable work for them, their owners turned them loose along the Gila, to the eastward of Yuma, where they have been living and breeding, looking fat and sleek all the time. For a while they were in danger of extermination. Whenever they put in an appearance along the wagon road, they frightened mules and horses beyond control of the drivers. They soon earned the everlasting hatred of teamsters, some of whom acquired a

---

[10] William B. Rhodes, also known as Roods and sometimes Rodes. Contemporary newspaper spelling was usually Roods. His rancho was known as Rancho de las Yumas and was located on the east bank of the Colorado River, between La Paz and Yuma. He owned a sixteen mile stretch of river frontage.

habit of shooting camels on sight. Since, however, the railroad has been delivering freight to Adonde's,[11] the road along the Gila this side of that place has been comparatively abandoned by teamsters, and the remaining camels have now a good chance to show what they can do in the way of propagation. The water-less desert of Sonora, south and southeast of Yuma, is known to posses immense deposits of salt, sulphur, borax, and soda; its mountains are also known to carry extensive deposits of metals. To these camels we look for eventually making treasures accessible and available.

Richard Van Valkenburgh [12] tells of how Fred Wright came to know about the camels in the desert from Yellow Dog, a name given an old prospector because he always had a yellow dog hanging around him. "Then Yellow Dog's camel story unraveled itself. There had been camels in the Sonoran desert. One of the band which had been brought down to the Sierra Pinta mines [13] by some Frenchmen, had turned up on the Sonoita River,[14] but it had vanished in the desert some years before Fred's arrival. Local natives recall the weird antics of this camel, who was known as Old Esau." Fred Wright's Treasure Map of southwest Arizona and northwest Mexico shows "Old Esau" near the Sierra Pinta Mountains.

Then on June 28, 1879, the *Sentinel* had the following:

While traveling recently across a desert south of the Gila, and many miles from that stream, we came across the figure of a

[11] Adonde is still a siding on the Southern Pacific Railroad, just west of Wellton, Arizona. Before the railroad, which was completed through here in January, 1879, Adonde was a stage stop, due to it's well water.

[12] Richard Van Valkenburgh, "His Compass Was a Burro's Tail," *Desert Magazine* (Sept. 1947).

[13] In southwestern Yuma County, Arizona.

[14] A small stream with headwaters in Pima County and in Sonora, Mexico. It provides water for the town of Sonoita, Sonora (which is two miles south of the International Border, below Organ Pipe National Monument in Arizona). The river flows southwestward from this town and disappears in the desert sands long before reaching the Gulf of California.

camel drawn upon the ground rudely, but with remarkable
accuracy, and on a scale six or eight times larger than life.
Evidently some Indian had seen a camel out there, and had
drawn this picture to put his experience on record. A few camels
were turned loose here some two or three years ago and have now
got scattered over the country as far as the vicinity of Tucson;
some of them having been tracked near that city.

The following was copied from the Tucson *Citizen*
by the *Sentinel* and published May 7, 1881.

WILD CAMELS IN ARIZONA

It is not generally known that camels roam over the desert
wastes of central and southern Arizona, but it is a fact, nevertheless. Many years ago – we believe it was in 1858 – a number
of camels were imported into Texas for use on the western plains,
where the scorching rays of the sun poured down on the sandy
desert and where water was to be had only at long intervals.
We are not advised as to the success of the undertaking on the
plains of Texas. The war coming on, the camels were either
sold or allowed to roam at large, and a portion of them found
their way into Arizona, and were used for a time in carrying
freight across the California desert. But for some cause or other,
perhaps from a want of knowledge as to the peculiar habits of
the animal, they did not prove profitable, and were turned loose
on the Gila and Salt River bottoms, where they continued to
remain. The old camels have brought forth young and multiplied,
until now they roam along the lower Gila in large numbers, and
seem to be contented and happy. The old ones are still tame,
but the younger generation is a little shy, not having been accustomed to the ways of men. The country seems to be peculiarly
adapted to the camel, and we have no doubt they will continue
to increase in numbers, until a drove of wild camels will become
as common on the western plains of Arizona as buffalo now are
on the plains of the Rocky Mountains.

The person who wrote this prophetic article described
the camel's situation very well except that he did not
forsee the near extinction of the buffalo and the camels.

We may well ask, for what reason were three independent camel caravans taken to Arizona instead of

setting the animals loose in the southern Nevada deserts? Certainly there were no mining operations in Arizona to amount to anything until the Silver King reached a stage of production approaching that of the Comstock Lode in 1876-77.

It has been noted that Samuel McCleneghan brought his dromedaries to Fort Yuma in 1866, where he died, leaving his half-brother LaFlamme, Hi Jolly, and Greek George stranded there. The camels disappeared into the Sonoran desert.

Laumeister arrived at Fort Yuma by vessel from Fort Mohave with fifty Bactrians in 1872, and not finding any employment for their use, apparently returned to Virginia City, again returning to Arizona in 1876.

The Chevaliers crossed the Colorado River to Fort Yuma in March, 1877, with thirty-six Bactrians and not finding any employment for them let them loose to wander up and down the Gila and Colorado rivers (newspaper version).

We have noted that two wagon trains drawn by mules brought 36,050 pounds of silver ore from the Silver King mine to Yuma in January, 1877, destined by vessel for San Francisco. Here we have a hint as to why camels were scarcely used in Arizona.

But we still have not found the answer as to why these camels were brought into Arizona in the first place, until we learn that thirty of them, driven by two Frenchmen, left Florence in 1876, bound for a mining camp in Sonora, Mexico. This could have been Laumeister's group, which would seem to indicate that his obituary, which stated that he had first arrived in Yuma about 1877, was in error. We also know that another caravan of twenty-eight camels left Florence in July, 1877, also led by two Frenchmen, very likely the Chevaliers. This would explain the newspaper question of their whereabouts two years later.

These two instances of camels being taken into Sonora to be engaged in mining operations may be just the reason the three owners took their animals into Arizona. Perhaps their intentions were to travel into Mexico, where gold, silver and copper mines had been in operation for at least three centuries by the Spaniards, and before that, by the Indians.

It was mining that first attracted the Spaniards northward from the Central Highlands onto the Meseta Central where wild and hostile Indians lived. They were mostly hunters and gatherers known as the Chichimecas. The Spaniards did not break through into the Chichimeca country until 1541, when several groups of Chichimeca Indians were defeated in the Mixton War [15] north of Guadalajara.

After the Mixton War, the Spanish miners moved quickly northward along the eastern and western edges of the Sierra Madre Occidental [16] to establish flourishing mining towns. Zacatecas, Guanajuato, Sombrerete, and many others, all began as important towns at or near the mines. The fabulous veins which are exposed in the shale sediments at Guanajuato made that city the richest mining community in the colonial New World. The recent opening of a massive silver mine in the State of Guanajuato will make Mexico the world's top silver producer.

In the Sierra Madre Occidental, veins at great depth were discovered in such abysmal canyons as

[15] Mixton is a mountain vastness the Chichimeca Indians retreated into, forcing the Spaniards into a long guerilla war.

[16] The spine of mountains which runs down the west side of northern Mexico for over a thousand miles, and creates the Continental Divide in that part of the country.

that of the Urique River (Barranca del Cobre), where silver, lead, zinc, and iron are all exposed in slates. Spanish miners preceded our modern "explorers" into this great barranca by centuries. The famous silver mines at Batopilas, Chihuahua, were discovered in a nearby deep canyon.

Some mines have been located in canyons cut by streams below the sterile surface of basalt or along the edges of the Central Highlands. Sites of the latter kind are found at Guanajuato, Taxco, and the old placer works on the Pacific slope in the state of Colima. Here the Indian and early colonial miners obtained gold, weathered out of quartz veins in rocks without a basalt cover. The Indians of the highlands mined and worked gold, copper, tin, and a little silver. The Spaniards appropriated these Indian mining areas and discovered new deposits. Silver became the most important mineral product of New Spain.

The value of silver was much greater than that of other minerals exploited, but gold mining was also important in the Sierra Madre Occidental. By the eighteenth century, many of the high-grade ores had been worked out. However, in the latter decades of the nineteenth century, industrial minerals increased in value relative to precious metals.

It is about 150 miles from Florence to Nogales on the Mexican border. Directly south from Nogales, Guanajuato is reached by way of the old Coronado Trail via Guaymas and Huatabampo (Sonora). At Guanajuato we go directly east to a region where several rivers form the Barranca del Cobre ("Canyon of the Copper"). Here are the Guanajuato mines, 400 miles from Nogales. The total distance from Florence, Arizona, to the Guanajuato mines is 550 miles. Another twenty-five miles brings us to the mines at Santa Bar-

bara. All of these locations are within the state of Chihuahua.

It would be impossible to record the fate of the Mexican ventures of two independent camel caravans without some authoritative records. As already stated, the production of these Mexican mines was rapidly declining in the late 1800s. The minerals were found in deep gorges of the Sierra Madre Occidental, and had to be brought up steep trails to the reduction mills.

We can assume the Bactrians were fully capable of transporting heavy loads of ore but that they would have difficulty climbing or descending the steep inclines, especially when rendered slippery from heavy rains and snows in the high mountain areas. There was also the matter of the drivers. Where peons or Indians were used, wages would be pitifully low, compared to those paid in the western United States. This would encourage low contractual payments to the owners of the camels. Instead of hauling up the ore, the camels may have been used to carry salt to the mills. All of this, of course, is highly conjectural. We cannot positively be certain of the fate of these caravans, nor can we know the absolute fates of either Laumeister or the Frenchmen.

A sympathetic writer once said,

> Poor camels, far from their natural habitat and not welcome except as harmless denizens of the range! Their strange odor and appearance stampeded all other animals on the road; their ungainly form did not lend itself to the cinches of the diamond hitch; the professional packer had little patience, nor did he pause at regular intervals to kneel and pray, as does the Turk or Mohammedan. The place for the camel in our literature of the inland empire is the so-called historical novel.

7

The Last Days of Hi Jolly and Greek George

It seems fitting to devote this final chapter to the two men who perhaps knew the camels best. The short review of Hi Jolly's life in *Camels to California,* by this writer, seems hardly enough, so we turn to the account of Roscoe Willson.[1]

Since the abandonment of McCleneghan's camels in 1866 at Fort Yuma, Hi Jolly seems to have been a happy-go-lucky fellow, not too fond of work, nor adhering closely to facts in his yarns. Dates meant nothing to him and apparently he jumbled them in his tales.

Fred Kuehn of Quartzsite who knew Hi Jolly intimately in his last years says that the camel driver was a short, dark, stocky man with a large bulbous nose. He had a friendly disposition and spoke very broken English. His Spanish was much better.

We hear of him in Arizona as being employed with General George Crook as a mule packer with the Army at various times and at various places. In 1880 he seems to have been employed with the Army near Tucson and about that time he became a naturalized citizen, taking the name of Philip Tedro.

It was in 1880 that he married Gertrudis Serna in Tucson and lived there for a time. In the early 1880's he is said to have been with the Army at Hauchuca and other posts until the surrender of Geronimo in 1886.

In the meantime he became the father of two girls, Amelia and Herminia, both born in Tucson.

About 1889, he became tired of domesticity and went prospecting in the desert, stopping with Tom Childs near Ajo for

---

[1] Willson, "Camels in Arizona and the West."

a time while he tried unsuccessfully to collect one or two of his old camels for transportation.

During this period he also stayed frequently with the Cullings at Cullings Well west of Wickenburg. Daniel Cullings Sr., who died in Phoenix several years ago, told the writer that Hi Jolly once brought in a quarter-grown camel calf and gave it to him. It finally wandered away and was never seen again.

In the ensuing years Hi Jolly made a precarious living at mining and prospecting, eventually establishing headquarters in a little cabin at Quartzsite.

His daughter, Herminia (Minnie) now Mrs. Hansford, says that about 1898 her father came through Tucson with a burro prospecting outfit, became ill at San Xavier and was taken to a Tucson hospital.

While in the hospital he asked Dr. Purcell to pursuade his wife and daughters to visit him. They complied, but when he asked his wife to take him back she refused.

Hi Jolly, then about 70, returned to Quartzsite where until his death December 16, 1902 [reported in error on page 87 in *Camels to California* as 1903], he was supported largely by merchant Mike Welz and other friends. Congressman Mark Smith tried to get him a pension but was unsuccessful.

He was buried in a simple grave with a wooden headboard and lay forgotten more than 30 years until James L. Edwards of the State Highway Department, had the handsome pyramid tomb erected in 1934. Then Hi Jolly the camel driver was given a big blowout with Governor B. B. Moeur and other bigwigs in attendance.

All the old prospectors in the desert region attended Hi Jolly's funeral and helped place him in the grave, over which the monument now stands. There were no flowers and no ceremony, since no preacher was available.

In *Camels to California* we gave brief reference to Greek George living in an adobe house in 1867, in what is now Hollywood. We now have a story connected with this house, as told by Don Juan or Eugene R. Plummer of "Señor Plummer," published in 1942 by the *Times-Mirror,* Los Angeles:

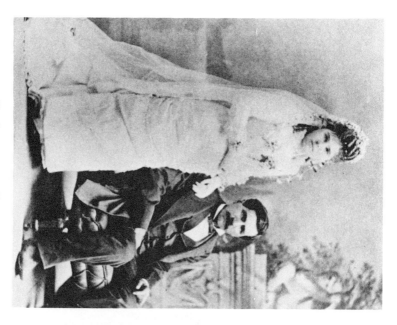

Hi Jolly and Bride

Camel driver Hi Jolly (Hadji Ali) who as Philip Tedro was married to Gertrudis Serna in Tucson in 1880. This photo was given to Roscoe Willson by Hi Jolly's daughter, Mrs. Herminia Hansford of Tucson.

Courtesy, Roscoe Willson.

Greek George Monument

Placed in dedication at the Pio Pico Mansion.

See page 149, herein.

"GREEK GEORGE"

BORN IN SMYRNA AS

GEORGE CARALAMBO

CAME TO THIS COUNTRY AS A
CAMEL DRIVER FOR THE
UNITED STATES GOVERNMENT
IN 1857

NATURALIZED—GEORGE ALLEN
IN 1867

DIED SEPT. 2, 1913 AT OLD MISSION

HISTORICAL MARKER ERECTED BY
WHITTIER PARLOR NO. 298
NATIVE DAUGHTERS OF THE GOLDEN WEST
COURTESY OF F. G. SIMONS AND R. D. WHITE
JUNE 30, 1956

We had a famous old character, Greek George, working for us on the ranch. Mother told the Greek to keep a lookout and next time the Land Shark made a trip across our place, to let her know.

The dance ended around midnight or a little after — it was a fine mootlight night I remember — we started home, Vasquez and some of his boys escorting Uncle Mike Lineres and me to a fork in the road.

Vasquez suddenly asked "Where's Greek George? Where is my Pariente?"

The old camel driver from Smyrna was supposed to have been one of the party guests, and Vasquez, who had cut all ties with relatives, liked to feel that George was a kind of "parent" and protector to him, therefore called him his "pariente." But it just struck him now, why hadn't the old man come to the dance?

Vasquez seemed to have a hunch that something was wrong. He turned to one of his men, Gregorio Lopez, and said, "Lopez, you gallop on down ahead and see if the Greek is home. But keep off the middle of the road, ride in the soft dirt along the side of the road so your horse won't be heard."

Lopez started off, and the bandit leader said to the rest of us, "George is a Greek, and I never knew one I could trust. Something's wrong. We'd better disband here."

They broke up at that, Vasquez starting toward Sherman, after Lopez. Uncle Mike Lineres and I said good-night and rode on east to our homes.

A reward of $8,000 had been posted for the capture of Tiburcio Vasquez, and it developed that Greek George had gone and turned state's evidence to collect that money [and] also got himself locked up for protection. His sister-in-law, Modesta Lopez, had a hand in the thing too, she was in love with Vasquez and jealous because he had a girl up at Hughes Lake that she could not make him forget.

Sheriff William R. Rowland and a posse of men were rendezvousing in a little shack I had built with drygoods boxes out on Section Eight in Sherman. They were waiting for a chance to swoop down on Vasquez and as many of his gang as he might have with him in Greek George's house.

Joe Manriquez came along, driving a wagon with a high box, to get a load of wood out of the canyon, and this was the chance the sheriff and his posse had been waiting for. They got in the waiting-box, lying down flat out of sight, and told Joe to drive to Greek George's [home].

The Lopez girl was watching from a window of the casita and they saw her signal, a handkerchief waved once over her shoulder, then they rushed the place. Her sister, Greek George's wife, was in bed sick in childbirth, so when Vasquez tried to get his weapons in the bedroom he found the door locked. He jumped through a back window and made for his horse.

Vasquez never reached his horse. He was brought down with nine slugs in him, from Emil Harris' guns. But he was not dead, in fact was still alive enough to be packed off to jail in the wagon of a next door neighbor, Vicente Valdez.

Born in Monterey, California, Tiburcio Vasquez learned early to hate the rough Americans who were everywhere elbowing the natives into obscurity. For fifteen out of twenty years of freebooting (five years he spent in San Quentin for horse stealing), he rode the back trails and highways of his native state at will, defying the sheriffs of several counties until, on May 14, 1874, he was captured. There was an $8000 reward for Vasquez if he was taken alive, and a $6000 reward if he was brought in dead. He was thirty-nine years of age at the time of his capture, and was executed on March 19, 1875.

On the news that Vasquez was captured and had been badly wounded, Greek George's heart went down to his boots. Sheriff Rowland hastened off to jail, incarcerated George and interned Tiburcio. Greek George was later released, to wed again. He did not lose his connection to Vasquez, according to the following from the Los Angeles *Herald,* June 11, 1900:

Memories of Escapades of
Tiburcio Vasquez
GREEK GEORGE WEDS
Greek George is married and another notch is cut in his historic

record. You don't know Greek George? Why, not to know, at least, of that one time-noted personage is to confess ignorance of some of the most notable events in the early history of Los Angeles, and, indeed, of the Golden state.

George Allen, so called because that is not his name, gave his age as 64, his place of nativity as Greece, and announced his intention last week of taking to wife one Concepcion Vajar, a native of Mexico, aged 57.

He is the Greek George of ancient history in whose house out on the Brea rancho[2] the bandit Vasquez was captured. Vasquez, the bandit! The admiration of the women, and the despair of the men – particularly the officers of the law. He who cut a throat or bestowed a benediction with an equally courtly grace, was betrayed in the house of his friend, and was made to ornament the gallows tree at San Jose.

What is now Hollywood Bowl became a part of Plummer's ranch. Nearby was Greek George's land, and he was in bad need of a little cash (1876). He sold the tract of 142 acres to Plummer, because he had the ready cash, of $450.00.

At one time it had been generally accepted that Greek George had killed a white man in New Mexico some ten years after coming to America (1867), and was later found dead on the plains. Some said he committed suicide rather than be captured, while others reported that he was killed by the Apaches.

It was with much surprise when one day in June, 1949, while researching at the Whittier Public Library, that this writer came across a news item that Greek George was buried in Whittier, California. I contacted the E. H. White Mortician, who searched their old card files and found that the burial plot was in Block 8, Lot I, Plot 6, in the old Mount Olive

[2] Also known as "Mitchell's Bee Ranch," it was leased to Greek George by Major Henry M. Mitchell. It was located on what is now the stage of the Hollywood Bowl. Frank F. Latta, *Saga of Rancho El Tejon* (Bear State Books, Santa Cruz, Ca., 1976).

Cemetery, now converted into a park. Sure enough, the old wooden headboard, in sad repair, was found among the trees and fallen limbs, covered with weeds.

A monument to the old camel driver was originally dedicated on June 30, 1956, but it was to be located at several places before its final resting place at the Governor Pio Pico Mansion in Whittier, on August 29, 1976.

The dedication was sponsored by the Governor Pico Mansion Society, by President Jayme Botello, at which six Greek dancers performed before an audience of over 100 people. Mildred McGee, Past President of Whittier Parlor No. 298, Native Daughters of the Golden West, made the Invocation. Later a tour of the Pico Mansion was conducted.

The size of the stone is about 36" high by 29" wide.

Greek George died at the age of 84. He had outlived his long associate, Hi Jolly, by nearly ten years.

Appendices

APPENDIX I

A Sequel to *Camels to California*

The photo of Edward Beale in *Camels to California* facing page 66, shows a man in his late forties. It was taken in San Francisco shortly after the end of the Civil War. We now have a miniature painting on ivory of Beale while serving in the Navy, made in 1846, at the age of twenty-four.

The sketch of Beale's Old Adobe at El Tejon facing page 67 of *Camels in California,* was probably made about 1860. The house was situated on a hill some 500 feet high, overlooking the valley. It is of interest to note that when Beale delivered his herd of camels to Fort Tejon in 1857, it was his first observation of the country with its considerable grass and wildlife. Shortly afterward Beale purchased 40,000 acres for five cents an acre from Spanish-Mexican absentee landowners who had little interest in such huge tracts of land.

A rare sketch here is "1857 – The Camel Express," accompanied by the comments: "Mutual distrust and dislike soon developed between the animals and the American mule drivers. Their vigorous invective and fierce commands shocked the sensitive feelings of the quadrapeds who seldom had heard any language more strenuous than the soft liquid syllables lisped in Arabian tongue. They balked at the rough treatment, as shown in the accompanying illustration, and refused to budge." (Page 146 herein).

We now have more information on McCleneghan's background. He had helped to care for Uncle Sam's camels at Camp Drum for several years before their sale by the government. Willson asserts McCleneghan met Beale's first caravan as it was setting out from Camp Verde for the Zuni Villages. Woodward notes that McLeneghan joined Lieutenant Joseph Ives in his survey of Death Valley in February of 1861, in which three camels were employed to carry half the supplies of food, instruments, and so on, fourteen men and twenty mules. And we do know McCleneghan died at Yuma in 1866, shortly after bringing his camels there.

Readers who wish to obtain a copy of *Camels to California,* which is out of print, may purchase an excellent reproduction, authorized by this writer, from University Microfilm, Ann Arbor, Michigan.

APPENDIX II

A Memorial to Beale's Camel Expedition

Of the thousands of tourists who leave Los Angeles via Highway 66 through San Bernardino and Barstow, across the Colorado River at Needles, south to Topock, Arizona, and through Kingman on their way to the Grand Canyon of Arizona, few realize they are going over the same route by which Edward Beale brought his caravan of 25 camels from San Antonio to Fort Tejon in 1857. It was near Kingman that his caravan passed on October 17th, on its way to cross the Colorado River.

The City of Kingman is a living memorial to that event, for the main street and a plaza through which Highway 66 passes are both named after Edward Beale. In this flagstone paved plaza is a high pyramidal, truncated monument, also built of native flagstone, on top of which is a parade of a camel caravan, an Army Cavalry and a covered wagon train around its periphery, with three large bronze plaques on three sides.

This memorial was conceived jointly by the Mohave County Chamber of Commerce at Kingman and the Arizona State Development Board. The plaza, monument, plaques and symbols were designed by the Engineering & Designing Division of the Arizona State Highway Department. It was dedicated in 1956, nearly a century after Beale's caravan passed through.

Kingman is a fairly large city of about 10,000 people, situated on a plateau some 3,300 feet above sea-level. A museum known as the Museum of History & Arts is operated by the Mohave Pioneers Historical Society, of which Dr. Paul V. Long was its first president, and to whom the writer is grateful for the photo of the monument.

About a mile north of the city is a preserved tract of land where Beale camped for several days to rest, preparatory to crossing the Colorado River.

The plaques on the monument read as follows:

EDWARD F. BEALE
Miniature painted on Ivory in 1846
showing Beale in Mexican garb.
Courtesy, Decatur House Museum,
Washington, D.C.

CAMELS AT FORT TEJON
Courtesy, Decatur House.

THE CAMEL EXPRESS, 1857
Courtesy, U.S. Federal Highway Administration.

EDWARD F. BEALE MEMORIAL

Photograph courtesy of Dr. Paul Long, Kingman, Az.

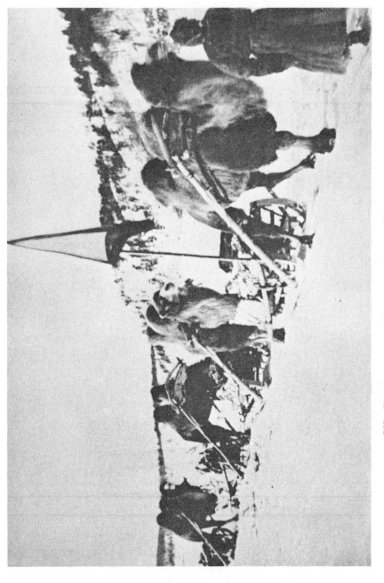

W. H. JACKSON'S PHOTOGRAPH OF BACTRIANS
This photo, taken on the Amur River, shows the camels
pulling sleds in frigid weather. See page 154.
Courtesy, Wm. H. Jackson, *Time Exposure*, Putnam & Sons, 1940.

Lt. Edward Fitzgerald Beale
1822 - 1893
Pioneer in the Path of Empire.
Hero of the War with Mexico.
Lieutenant in United States
Navy. Appointed General by
The Governor of California.
Commanded Exploration of Wagon
Route to the Colorado River
With the Only Camel Train in
American History 1857-1858.

Wagon Route
Surveyed by Lt. Edward F. Beale
1857-1858. Followed by Railroad
Survey 1858-1859. Route of
Atlantic and Pacific Railroad
Built Across Arizona 1882-1883.
Tracks Reached Kingman Spring
1883. U.S. Highway 66 Closely
Follows Beale's Survey.

United States Army
Established Camp Beale's Spring
About One Mile North, March 25,
1871 for the Protection of
Settlers and Travelers on
Northern Route. Served as
Haulapai Indian Agency. Military
Camp Abandoned April 6, 1874.

The Fort Mohave Site was beside the Colorado River seven miles north of the town of Topock, on Interstate Route 40. The elevation is 510 feet, a drop of over 2,800 feet from Kingman in a distance of sixty miles. A plaque embedded in a large boulder reads as follows:

Old Fort Mohave
Western Anchor of a Military
Road Across Northern Arizona.
Near here in 1858 Beale's Camel
Expedition was Ferried Across
The Colorado River on the Steamer
General Jessup. The Fort was

Abandoned at the start of the
Civil War. Was Activated Again
in 1863, and then in 1880 Assigned
To Civilian Use of the Fort
Mohave Indian Reservation.

About forty miles east of Kingman, on Highway 66, is the town of Truxton, named after Beale's son. Highway 66 continues on to Albuquerque, New Mexico, where, it is said, Samuel McCleneghan joined the expedition. Of course Hi Jolly and Greek George were already busy with the dromedaries at this place.

APPENDIX III

An Unsolved Photograph of a Camel Train

Ever since the Dromedaries and Bactrians were introduced in the western United States, few photos of the animals in their natural state have been found, a fault frequently lamented by historians.

As noted in *Camels to California,* Beale had a photographer from San Antonio take some pictures for the Secretary of the Interior. This writer has personally made fruitless searches at the National Archives in Washington for these photos, and others have found the same situation.

With few exceptions, pictures of camels were shown in sketches executed by Edward Vischer, Ernest Narjot, and other artists.

It was therefore with much surprise that in Roscoe Willson's serial of "Camels in Arizona," a photograph of a camel train appeared in which some thirty Bactrians were shown crossing what appears to be rocky land. This photo was found by Paul Ullman of the Crest Book Store in Phoenix, who had no idea when or where it was taken. Mr. Willson kindly gave this writer a copy of the photo, with permission to use it, and it appears as the frontispiece in this work.

It is a photo that must have been taken back in the 1860's or 1870's by a photographer equipped with a camera which had rapid movement, and which could produce size and clarity. Stanley Paher's book contained over 700 photographs, many of them taken by photographers betwen 1860 and 1870. The pictures are evidence that, by that time, camera technology was sufficiently evolved to render clear and detailed prints. The photo of the camel crossing was probably once set in a frame and kept in a well-protected home or office.

A careful inspection shows the following interesting facts:

1. The animals seemed well trained and are walking along at a steady gait. They are all of mature age as noted by their huge size.

2. As shown by their heavy hairy manes, these are Bactrians.

3. They are joined by a rope leading from their nose to the saddle of the forward camel. A rope is seen to extend from the left camel to another one outside of the picture.

4. It appears that seven camels were thus held to a separate group, and that the train was composed of four groups for a possible total of twenty-eight animals. But there appears to be more than that number. The count is made difficult as the train seems to be turning to the left far up front.

5. The photo gives the impression that the caravan has been, or is going, on a long journey across a waste of land, perhaps a dry river bed between mountainous terrain.

6. As indicated by the large pan-like appearance of their feet, the camels are protected by some form of leather or canvas pads, similar to those used in Laumeister's caravan.

7. It appears that the five camels of the nearest group carried ore or salt in heavy white sacks or rolls, and some matted material between the humps. The other two camels of the same group seem to be carrying long bundles of wooden sticks. Some of the singularly packed camels may be carrying camping and cooking utensils.

8. In the right foreground is the shadow of a man in heavy clothes, behind whom was the photographer. Certainly they were not far from some community.

9. Only one driver is seen up front. The man in the shadow may be another driver.

Now the question arises, where was this remarkable photo taken?

1. At Walla Walla? No, because there were only 18 Bactrians, according to James Watt.

2. At Virginia City, Nevada? Thirty camels were reported seen in 1869, many of them young. Doubtful.

3. Probably used on the Union Pacific Railway to lay eighty miles of tracks from Humboldt Wells eastward? The ties were eight feet long, eight inches wide and six inches thick, of roughly cut timber, and are not shown in this photo. Very doubtful.

4. At Austin? Bactrians were there for many years. We do not know if they were used in long trains or in groups of seven. The *Reese River Revielle* may have had a photographer. Very possible.

5. At Fort Yuma? The reporter saw thirty-six Bactrians. He may have seen them in caravan form before they reached Yuma. He may also have taken pictures for the *Arizona Sentinel* in 1877. But why would they be carrying salt or ore, since they must have arrived nearly empty of freight from Nevada? Doubtful.

6. At Florence, Arizona? A news reporter says he saw thirty camels leave the town for Sonora in 1876. They may have been used for packing ore to Yuma previous to that date. Quite possible.

7. Used in movies? All movies, especially *Lawrence of Arabia,* used Dromedaries. And if movies were set in the Mideast, these species were used. Bactrians are rare in that country. Not so.

The reader must make his choice.

An American Sees Long Bactrian Caravans
in India and Siberia

William Henry Jackson, the famous photographer whose pictures of the old and new world taken between 1860 and '70 are now known world wide, wrote his autobiography, *Time Exposure,* in 1940, at the remarkable age of eighty years.

Jackson was one of five members of the World's Transportation Commission of the Field Columbian Museum of New York City, which left October 3, 1894, on a tour which lasted seventeen months. They visited Europe, Northern Africa, and parts of India, encircled Australia, and penetrated the Orient.

On February 5th, 1894, on a cold, clear day, the party arrived at Peshawar, India, and saw the Hindu Kush Mountains. They were taken by two-wheeled carts through the famous Khyber Pass of ancient history. Here Jackson related the following: "On the way up the gorge we overtook a two-mile caravan of camels bearing great boxes and bags of rock salt to Kabul. If it had been ordered for our pleasure, it could not have been no more picturesque. And, I am sure, if the caravan had passed 500 years before, it could have differed in no important detail – except that archers would have guarded it, instead of Khyber Rifles."

These animals were surely Bactrians, for the Khyber Pass was the entrance into what is today the Soviet Union and China.

Then in November of 1895, the five men crossed the Amur River at Khabarovsk and traveled in the direction of Nikolsk. Nearly all the way was over thick, smooth ice, black as ink in some places.

They arrived in Albazin soon after midnight on the twentieth, and taking advantage of a brilliant moonlight pressed on toward China. At this point Jackson relates, "Near Petrovskaya, I saw and photographed one of the most extraordinary sights of my whole trip around the world – a caravan of camels drawing sledges. There were a thousand or more shaggy Bactrians in line, and accustomed as they were to the rigors of the Siberian winter, many of the beasts were nevertheless bleeding at the nostrils from the cold. It was 25° below zero when I took my pictures."

The photo on page 148 shows the most unusual sight of heavily loaded sledges being pulled by long bamboo poles secured to the forward hump of the Bactrian. And it does appear that their feet were shod in leather shoes. The Russian army may have adopted the use of sledges as a means of stabilizing the camel on slippery ice, and relieving drivers of the awkward strapping of military supplies over the two humps. Abbe Huc noted that the carriages of the kings and princes were drawn by camels, and were sometimes harnessed to palanquins.

Jackson added that, where the ground had been blown almost clean of snow, the men were transported in a four-wheeler, but that, when they encountered snow once more, they were switched to their sledges, which had been hauled over the bare ground behind extra horses.

The fact that Jackson saw thousands of Bactrians hauling supplies in India and Siberia makes one realize how ridiculously small in number were the camel caravans used in western America.

APPENDIX V

Civilian Operation of Camel Trains in Western America

We have set in graphic form the movements of the five civilian owners of camel caravans in Western America.

Two groups came from the U.S. Army Camel Corps at Camp Verde, Texas: Samuel McCleneghan in California and Bethel Coopwood in Texas.

A group of eighty-nine camels imported by Mrs. M. J. Watson into Galveston, Texas, and after a year of care at the Lubbock Ranch at Houston, Texas, were turned loose.

Two groups from Julius Bandmann of San Francisco, Cal: Louis Chevalier of Nevada, and Frank Laumeister in Canada.

Three of these eventually entered Yuma, Arizona, after crossing the Colorado River, and two of them continued on to the mines in Sonora, Mexico, but very possibly ending at the great silver mines at Guanajuato in Northern Mexico.

There are no records of the Chevalier Brothers' lives in Mexico, but there is a strong indication that Laumeister returned to Yuma and lived the rest of his life in that city.

Civilian Operations of Camel Trains in Western America

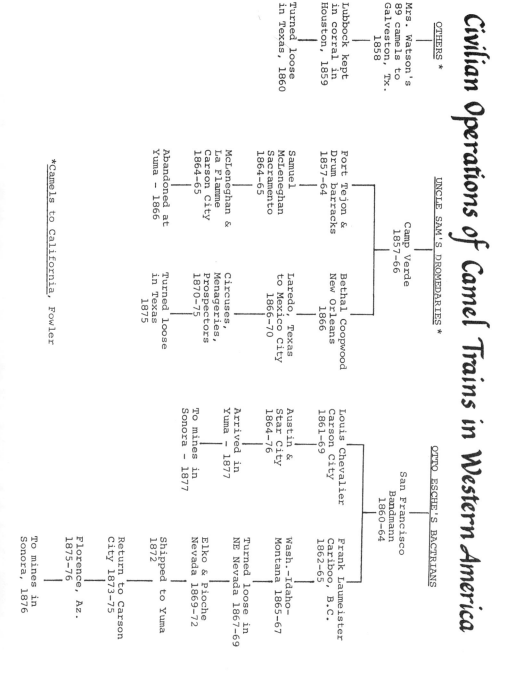

OTHERS *

Mrs. Watson's
89 camels to
Galveston, Tx.
1858

Lubbock kept
in corral in
Houston, 1859

Turned loose
in Texas, 1860

UNCLE SAM'S DROMEDARIES *

Camp Verde
1857-66

Fort Tejon &
Drum barracks
1857-64

Bethal Coopwood
New Orleans
1866

Samuel
McLeneghan
Sacramento
1864-65

Laredo, Texas
to Mexico City
1866-70

McLeneghan &
La Flamme
Carson City
1864-65

Circuses,
Menageries,
Prospectors
1870-75

Abandoned at
Yuma - 1866

Turned loose
in Texas
1875

OTTO ESCHE'S BACTRIANS

San Francisco
Bandmann
1860-64

Louis Chevalier
Carson City
1861-69

Frank Laumeister
Cariboo, B.C.
1862-65

Austin &
Star City
1864-76

Wash.-Idaho-
Montana 1865-67

Arrived in
Yuma - 1877

Turned loose in
NE Nevada 1867-69

To mines in
Sonora - 1877

Elko & Pioche
Nevada 1869-72

Shipped to Yuma
1872

Return to Carson
City 1873-75

Florence, Az.
1875-76

To mines in
Sonora, 1876

*Camels to California, Fowler

Acknowledgements

I must not forget to acknowledge some of the chief contributors who made it possible to fill in important missing gaps in the entire camel episode.

The chief material on Otto Esche's experiences and the *Dollart* came from A. A. Gray's article in the *California Historical Society Quarterly,* Volume IX, Number 4, December, 1930.

Arthur Woodward's little book, *Camels and Surveyors in Death Valley,* supplied data and photographs not heretofore available to this writer on events in California and Arizona.

The main source of information on the Cariboo experience came from the Provincial Archives, Victoria, British Columbia. I am very grateful to Mr. W. E. Ireland, librarian and archivist, for his time-consuming efforts to help me unravel many missing links, and particularly for the biography of Frank Laumeister, who originated the idea of importing Bactrians into that country.

Art Down's excellent research on the Cariboo Trail and gold rush country proved invaluable.

Another principal source of information on camels in the northwestern United States was the Washington State Historical Society of Tacoma, Washington. Mr. Frank Green, librarian, supplied photocopies of the William S. Lewis and James W. Watt articles on camels in the Washington, Idaho, and Montana areas.

The almost total lack of information on the camels in Arizona in my first book, *Camels to California,* has been corrected by Mr. Roscoe Willson's series of articles which appeared in the *Arizona Republic,* Phoenix, in 1966. It is to Willson that I am indebted for the anonymous photograph of a huge camel train in the desert, and a rare photo of Hi Jolly and his wife, taken in 1880.

Mr. Joseph Miller of Phoenix, Arizona, supplied numerous news items on camels at Yuma in 1877 and afterward.

Dr. Paul V. Long, first President of the Mohave Pioneers Historical Society, rendered valuable photographs and data concerning the City of Kingman, Arizona, honoring Edward Beale's camel expedition through that area in 1857.

I also gratefully acknowledge the many contributions from the following sources: California State Library, Sacramento; Washoe County Library, Reno, Nevada; Nevada Historical Society, Reno, Nevada; Nevada State Library, Carson City, Nevada; Oregon Historical Society, Portland, Oregon; Eastern Washington State Historical Society, Spokane, Washington; Spokane Public Library, Spokane, Washington.

Also of tremendous assistance were: Montana Historical Society, Helena, Montana; Division of State History, Salt Lake City, Utah; Washington State Library, Olympia, Washington; Penrose Memorial Library, Walla Walla, Washington; Mr. Donald Powell, University of Arizona, Tucson, Arizona; Mrs. Margaret S. Bret Harte of the Arizona Historical Society in Tucson, who found Laumeister's obituary in a Yuma newspaper; Elko County Library; Mrs. Ruth Hoskins in Elko, Nevada; Mrs. Philip Radford, La Habra,

California; United State Department of Transportation, Washington, D.C.; Burlingame Public Library, Burlingame, Cal., supplied Abbe Huc's two volumes of his travels, William Jackson's *Time Exposure,* the diary of Robert Eccleston of Laumeister's time at Mariposa, Stanley Paher's *Nevada Ghost Towns,* and numerous other articles.

Bibliography
and Index

Bibliography

Ames, Charles Edgar. *Pioneering the Union Pacific.* N.Y: Appleton Century Crofts, 1968

Athearn, Robert G. *Union Pacific Country.* N.Y: Rand McNally and Company, 1971

Bailey, Richard. "The Camels." Manuscript in the Kern County Museum, Bakersfield, Ca: 1949

Crampton, C. Gregory. *The Mariposa Indian War, 1850-1851. Diaries of Robert Eccleston.* Salt Lake City: Univ. of Utah Press, 1957

Ginsburgh, Robert. "The Camels Are Coming." *American Legion Monthly* (January, 1928)

Huc, Regis-Evariste and Joseph Gabet. *Travels in Tartary, Thibet and China, 1844-46.* Tr. by William Hazlitt. N.Y: Harper and Brothers, 1928

Hunter, J. Marvin. *Old Camp Verde, the Home of the Camels.* Bandera, Tx: 1948

Jackson, William Henry. *Time Exposure.* N.Y: G. P. Putnam's Sons, 1940

Lewis, Oscar. *The Town That Died Laughing.* Boston: Little, Brown and Company, 1955

Lomax, Alfred L. "Brother Jonathan: Pioneer Steamship of the Pacific Coast." *Oreg. Hist. Soc. Qtly.* (September, 1959)

Lord, Eliot. *Comstock Mining and Miners, 1883.* Republished by Howell North, 1959

McDonald, Douglas B. "The Camels Are Coming." *The West* (Feb., 1967)

Miller, James P. *The Road to Virginia City* (Montana), 1960

Murbarger, Nell. *Ghosts of the Adobe Walls.* Los Angeles: Westernlore Press, 1964

Paher, Stanley W. *Nevada Ghost Towns and Mining Camps.* Berkeley: Howell North Books, 1970

Powell, Fred Wilbur, "Hall Jackson Kelly – Prophet of Oregon."
    Oreg. Hist. Qtly. (March, 1917)
Rister, Carl Coke. "When Camels Came to Texas." *Southwest
    Review* (Fall, 1945)
Van Valkenburgh, Richard. "His Compass Was A Burro's Tail."
    Desert Mag. (Sept., 1947)
Willson, Roscoe G. "Camels in Arizona and The West." *Arizona
    Republic* (March 6 - April 4, 1966)
Woodward, Arthur. *Camels and Surveyors in Death Valley.* Palm
    Desert, Ca: Desert Printers, Inc., 1961

Index

Compiled by Robert A. Clark